Cast from the Edge

Cast from the Edge
Tales of an Uncommon Fly Fisher

by
Scott Sadil

Greycliff Publishing Company
Helena, Montana

The following chapters appeared in slightly different form in *California Fly Fisher*: "The Ugly Emerger," "Beneath the Boarderlands," "Building Good Rods Cheap," and "Good as Gold."

© 1999 by Scott Sadil

Cover art: *Surf Fishing*, © by Shirley Cleary, Helena, Montana
Cover design by Geoffrey Wyatt, Helena, Montana
Typeset in Garamond and Humanst 521 by Geoffrey Wyatt, Helena, Montana
Printed by Thomson-Shore, Inc., Dexter, Michigan

10 09 08 07 06 05 04 03 02 01 00   10 9 8 7 6 5 4 3 2 1

Library of Congress Cataloging-in-Publication Data

Sadil, Scott.
         Cast from the edge : tales of an uncommon fly fisher / by Scott Sadil.
                 p.   cm.
         ISBN 1-890373-07-9 (alk. paper)
         1. Fly fishing—West (U.S.) Fiction. 2. Fishers—West (U.S.) Fiction.
3. Fishing stories, American. I. Title.
PS3569.A2375C37   1999
813'.54—dc21   99-39216
                                                                        CIP

This one is for my father.

CONTENTS

Then something quite primitive takes over and you leap off the cliff with your art, which your life begins to follow around like an orphan or waif follows his beloved dog.

—Jim Harrison

Creeps and idiots cannot conceal themselves for long on a fishing trip.

—John Gierach

A False Preface

*T**his book* was compiled from the journals of the legendary West Coast fly-fishing guru Francis Theodore Sepic. The journals themselves were presented to me along the great man's beloved North Fork, near the Glory Hole.

"I always thought I had no reason to share these," Sepic explained. "I was wrong."

Yet it's difficult to place this work in the context of a real man's life. "Any story told twice," said Grace Paley, "is fiction." In sharp contrast to his precise elegant prose, Francis Sepic's life remains mired in rumor, hearsay, and mystique. Certainly, the greatest distortions regard Sepic's fishing abilities: he is a mediocre caster, improbably traditional, and often painfully rough at the vise. But to hear others tell it, Francis Sepic the fly fisherman is a master, a virtuoso, a magician, or worse, a man who once dealt the devil his soul.

Years back, in Baja California, while fighting a good corvina toward the beach, the sort of fly-rod sport that eventually inspired my own book, *Angling Baja*, I was approached by two young surfers, boards under their arms, racing across the sand as if the waves were six-foot, perfect, and empty. In fact, the surf was flat—which was why I was fishing. Beyond the beach in the dunes, I spotted the kids' truck, a hint of dust still hanging in the shimmering heat. The first vulture had arrived, circling the edge of the mesa. I thought I could also see two girls near the truck, clued by the abrupt demarcation of bikini tops or untanned, naked breasts, fashionable, if infrequent in those parts. But it was often difficult in Baja to discern illusion from reality.

The two surfers stopped short of me, rising to their toes as they entered the cool water. I slid the corvina onto the sandbar, not yet covered by the tide, and freed the hook from its toothy mouth and returned it to the wash. I already had meat in camp. The surfers stood watching me, whispering between each other, ankle-deep in the hole I would be fishing at high tide. I waved and nodded.

"Sepic?" one finally said. "Francis Sepic?"

"Nope," I replied, shrugging my shoulders. "You've got the wrong guy."

Now, I had already heard about Francis Sepic. You would have to have been deaf, dumb, or traveling in a Winnebago not to. But until this chance meeting, he sounded like the sort of middle-aged burnout you encounter all around the world along the margins of surf—a Mickey Dora, say, in France, or Tony "Ant" Van der Heuwel at Jeffreys Bay, South Africa. I had never spoken to anyone who had actually met him. I hadn't even heard he fished.

"We thought you were Francis Sepic," said one of the boys. "We saw the fly rod and thought you were him."

They related a time two years before, just as a chubasco broke loose from the tropics, when they caught this same break at a solid eight feet, thin-lipped barrels winding all the way into town. I can't tell you how often I've heard that story. On occasion, I've had excuse to tell it myself. Yet *this* episode included a huge school of big fish—jacks, yellowtail, flashes of bull dorado—that parked itself just outside the point, encircling a wad of bait, scores of pelicans raining like spears from the sky.

"I was scared a bill would stick right through my fucking board!" shared one of the surfers.

Then Sepic arrived. Remarkably, he didn't paddle out. Instead, he headed down the beach with a fly rod, and he intercepted one of the boys rushing back toward the point, following yet another mile-long ride.

They struck a deal. In exchange for a joint of Escondido buds, Sepic had one of the kids take the fly in his teeth and paddle out with it beyond the break, into the maelstrom of birds, bait, and big fish. That seemed reasonable to me. My only real surprise was why I hadn't thought of the ploy myself. But this was Francis Theodore Sepic—not you or me or the multitude of other common fly rodders. Sepic, you see, wanted to present the fly "properly," the sort of vague, yet radiant concept you will find sprinkled throughout his writing. In this case, what that meant was the use of an oversized box kite to lift the two-hundred-yard entirety of his shooting head, running line, and backing, allowing the offshore right-hand wind to carry the fly down in line with the surf, loading the rod until the kite broke free, a loop formed in the line and gracefully unfolded, and Sepic executed a roll cast of Herculean dimensions—backhand, no less. I'm not precisely sure how it all worked. Most of us have trouble with Einstein, too.

It took Sepic and both surfers most of the afternoon to execute the cast. They kept losing the kite down the beach, then one of the kids would have to ride a wave all the way inside, and part of the deal was another joint each time the fly was paddled beyond the break. Sepic himself never smoked anything other than Camels those days. He was well aware, however, of the deeper motives of young surfers. Then, at sunset, just as the wind was quieting, the boys and Sepic put it all together, the line laid out like flight in a dream, and almost instantly Sepic was tight to God knows what.

"Son of a bitch!" he shouted, taking off down the beach at a dead run.

In the morning, he was still there. The surf had dropped, and Sepic stood silhouetted by the dawn light, motionless as a driftwood sculpture, a circle of cigarette butts around his feet. Occasionally, the subtlest of quivers ran through the length of the deep bend in his rod. The kids rushed down from their camp, exhaling smoke across the sand.

"It's probably a shark," said Sepic, shrugging his tensed shoulders. "But you never know."

One of the surfers held out a lit joint, offering Sepic a hit. He was tired, hungry, and tempted. But just then, the ocean moved, a broad swirl formed in the languid tide, and the spiny rays of resplendent fins—pectoral, dorsal, caudal—crossed the window in the surface as the great fish rolled, gently as true pleasure through a lover's soul.

"That's no fucking shark, sir!" observed one of the stoned boys. He turned to his pal, spread his arms wide in the manner of all big fish stories told, and the ember of the glowing joint brushed the stretched, taut head of Sepic's fly line.

"Oh, fuck," Sepic said.

The rod stood up straight. The pearlescent fly line fell to the sand and began sliding toward the water. The boy who had burned the line screamed and dived forward and tried to grab it. Sepic stepped after him. He reached out the length of the rod and rapped the boy firmly across the ear.

"Leave it," he said.

"But, but sir—"

"Leave it!" Sepic repeated. The tail of the severed line slithered into the water, disappearing in the lapping shore break. "If you don't do it right, it doesn't count."

Sepic helped the boy to his feet. He asked him for a light. He'd been rationing smokes throughout the night, only to come up one match short. He was dying for the last one.

"It doesn't matter," he said, striking the match on the reel seat.

"What about the fish?" asked the boy. "Won't the hook, the line—?"

"It'll work itself loose," said Sepic. He inhaled deeply. "I'll probably snag it at high tide."

Sepic and the two boys stood gazing out at the quiet water. A little set came through, immaculate six-inch waves spiraling just beyond the edge of the sand, a breath of wind lifting spray off the tops. Three pelicans swung in off the open sea around the point, and one of them suddenly wheeled and dived, hitting the surface

with an audible crash. Sepic sighed from the bottom of his heart.
"I guess it wasn't meant to be," he said.

It was Sepic himself who supplied me with the details of this
remarkable tale. Upon our fateful meeting along the North Fork, I
decided to ditch plans for the week, and I joined Sepic at what he
calls the Cathedral Camp, a splendid spot with miles of great
stream in either direction. We fished, of course—yet Sepic was
more intent on trying to sort out the behavior of his horren-
dously energetic, high-strung Chesapeake Bay retriever, Lucy. No
longer was Sepic trying to discipline or restrain her along the
bank while he fished. He had come to believe, he explained, that
the only way their relationship would work was if Lucy understood the goal of the sport and *chose* to behave with quiet
patience in accordance with the common good.

I have never suffered so many excellent fishing opportunities ruined as I did that week. Still, it was the chance to fish and
speak directly with Francis Sepic that spirited me away from
family and business. A few trout either way won't make a difference in any of our lives. Downstream from us, where the North
Fork joins the big river, becoming a Mecca for fly fishers in pursuit of all manner of trophies—steelhead, hog rainbows, and
occasionally, hatchery salmon—the vile lusts and incertitudes
that propelled Sepic beyond even the cultic limelight of the
sport remain in high season. Tucked away in the sort of obscure,
modest, yet glorious setting that Sepic has spent a lifetime
uncovering, we enjoyed a spell of mild spring weather, with just
enough rain to keep the currents full, the fish venturesomely on
the feed. At night, we sat talking long into the darkness, the
smoke of smoldering wet cedar lifting through the trees. Sepic's
story, it turned out, shared unnerving similarities with my own—
even down to the name of his longtime fishing buddy, Peter, so
that at times I suffered an acute sense of dislocation, as if my life
belonged to someone else. I began to suspect that there was

more at work here than chance, even perhaps, that I needed to understand Sepic's fly-fishing career if I was going to understand the direction of mine. As we talked, we shared Sepic's best cigars, and we sipped at a tea he called Hope, a rank concoction made of salal berries, fern spore, the bark of the madrona, and assorted seeds of various rare Cascadian wildflowers. But it did seem to calm down the dog some.

Near completion of *Angling Baja*, I shared another encounter with the presence of Francis Sepic—at least his presence in the aspect of a body. As spirit, he gained angling ascendancy down the length of the peninsula, just as he has come to be felt throughout the entire watershed of the northeastern Pacific. But in those days, Sepic was known as little more than another crack surfer gone to seed—small, lean, prematurely gray with a bristly, sun-damaged crewcut that looked more like fur than hair. There was always word about him fly fishing in the surf, but the reports seemed tinged by multifarious sentiment, as if inspired by eccentricity, instead of sport.

I was heading out across the Vizcaino desert with my close pal, Peter Syka, making for a secret mangrove we had heard about that was rumored still to contain the near-mythic black snook. It was June, a cold month along the Baja Pacific, the stiff onshore breezes mixing with thermal fogs, draping everything in a film of dampness that sucks the heat from your core. In some stretches of these western maritime deserts, this is the only form of precipitation that falls for years. It can make for a gray, desolate camp—a cross between the Nevada badlands and, say, western Wyoming—if you can't push on out to the beach before sunset, the misery quotient outweighed only by the wholesale dangers of driving in Baja at night. We stopped the truck in the middle of nowhere, heated up a can of refried beans to go with tortillas, beer, and the blowing sand, then spread out tarps and sleeping bags and crawled off into the night, descending into that special gloom for which the peninsula has long been famous.

I was awakened by something pulling my hair and the press of a blade edge tight against my throat. Peter looked like I was looking in a mirror. A handful of other figures stood ghostly about the camp, their faces inside ski masks and nylon stockings. I gave up and waited to die.

"*Sepic!*" said a voice behind me. "El que demonios da, diablos recibe!"

"I'm not Sepic!" I shouted.

"Fuck you," said the voice.

The hidden faces started laughing, the quintessence of the Mexican sense of humor. Two figures were shoved brusquely before me, the shape of a woman and a small child. Hands reached out and peeled back their masks.

"El tiempo cura y nos mata!"

The voice remained behind me, close to one ear, the blade hard to my neck against the pounding of my blood. I don't know how I didn't cry. I stared into the faces of a young woman and a girl, a toddler really, their dark hair and features the same, their expressions blank and infinite, eyes opaque, the elder's a shade deeper than the child's. My hair was pulled tighter still.

"*Sepic!*" said the voice behind me again. "*Sepic!* Fuck you!"

The young woman shook her head, her black eyes swallowing mine. She held my gaze an instant, then spit it to the ground, her full, blank expression unmoving. The little girl's eyes, pure as a new moon, lingered gently upon mine.

"I'm not Sepic," I said, and raised my eyes and arms, palms upward, toward the hazy stars.

Peter and I were released. The figures vanished as if coyotes stealing trash. A strange, soft tremble passed through camp, the sound of a breaking wave carried through fog—or a lover's laughter concealed by the beating of a heart.

"Go home," said the voice beyond us. "Go home!"

"*Did* you?"

Francis Sepic was fiddling with his leader and two flies, a big stone nymph and an oversized caddis, tied on a fine-wire size-10 Wilson fly hook from Partridge of Redditch. We were down on the Glory Hole, waiting for the sunlight to climb out of the tree-tops, on the last evening of my stay. Lucy lay spent at our feet, and I'd finally gotten up the nerve to tell Sepic the story, broach a cer-tain subject, if you will—although holding out until it's now or never is hardly an act of courage.

"*Did* you?" repeated Sepic, gauging the length of leader between the point fly and junction to the dry dropper. "Did you go home? Or did you stay and go fishing?"

"What do you think?" I asked, suddenly put off by Sepic's tone. It can get that way after a week together, no matter how much alike two fishermen think. It can get that way a lot sooner than that. "It's not like we made that trip every week."

"Did you get your *robalo*?" Sepic took the nail clippers hang-ing from his vest and trimmed the tag end of the clinch knot at the dropper, inspecting his work. Then he looked me straight in the eye, holding me with an intensely gentle smile. "If you did, I didn't read about it."

I shook my head. "The locals said they've netted all the snook—same as everywhere. We got mostly halibut and bay bass. And one white seabass over in the surf."

Sepic raised an eyebrow.

"Past Francisco's place?"

"Uh huh," I said. "It was flat, and you could get out on that little finger of rocks at high tide."

"That's the spot."

Looking back, I am certain Francis Sepic led me through this conversation, to the point where, naturally, I would mention the young woman and the child in the middle of nowhere and the desolate Baja night. In a world of perfect metaphors, I rose directly to the fly.

"Was she your daughter?" I asked.

Sepic stepped into the stream.

"I've slept a lot of places," he said.

He stripped handfuls of line off the reel, then roll cast down into the tailout, the awkward loop turning over slowly.

"If it happened, it's how it should be. There are no accidents."

Sepic always knew there were big fish in the Glory Hole. But he had never caught one, never seen or heard of one caught by anybody else. He liked to fish the pool from bottom to top with a little nondescript nymph dead drifted upstream right beneath the film. I had watched him catch a number of ten-inch and twelve-inch fish there, which was one size up from anything I managed to fool. Mostly, though, it was someplace to end the day quietly, throwing long, pointless casts that drifted back undisturbed, fainter and fainter as the shade turned to night.

But this was different. Sepic had a plan. He moved up into the pool, lobbing the two big flies straight across, figuring out what he could and couldn't do with them. Then he slid his hand down off the edge of the cane, fully onto the grip, and he sort of aimed and heaved and body-Englished a big, goofy loop far up and completely across the pool, smack dab onto an old black snag stuck a body's length out over the stream.

"A little trick I learned in seminary school," he said, one eyebrow raised.

Sepic lifted the line barely taut, the nymph staying put, the big dry dropper falling precisely to the stream. It hung there, dancing directly above the surface, moved by the slow current, air, I don't know what. Sepic took a deep breath. He straightened his back, flexing a moment inside his vest and waders, and then he exhaled slowly, as if emptying himself. He began waiting. For awhile I thought he was kidding. He looked a lot like a bait fisherman, the good ones who keep their minds right there with what's going on in the water. But then I noticed his eyes were closed, his breathing as slow and steady as the stream around his knees, and a couple of times I wondered if he were maybe sleeping, if he had dozed off, or something. The darkness grew more and more real, the light and the stream and the trees all blending into one, and I had a strange, awful sense of what it would be like to not know who you are—or to get lost while going nowhere.

I lost track of both Sepic and time. I think I was in the stream, but I'm not sure. The darkness was everywhere. Then there was a moment of brilliant light, a flash that receded instantly to the spot at which I'd been watching the dangling fly. The fish came crashing through the surface as if a work of delicate blown-glass art bursting through a window.

"There it is," said Sepic, his face lit up, too.

The fish took off downstream, Sepic's line running up, around, and *over* the snag.

"What now?" I asked.

"I don't know," said Sepic, wading off into deep water, Lucy closing in from behind. Then Sepic turned, his pale eyes catching mine, his intense, gentle smile spreading.

"You tell me. You're the hot-fuck fishing writer."

The rest was in the journals. Despite the enormity of the task, every effort has been taken to retain the author's intent, vision, and wisdom.

Francis Sepic is thought to be living and fishing in the greater Northwest.

—Scott Sadil

From the Journals
of Francis Theodore Sepic

First Season
Part One
FROM SEPIC'S JOURNALS

I'll take my chances and confess right off I moved here from California. My wife grew up in Madrone, Oregon, which should count for something, but I know it doesn't. I'm *one of them*, part of that perverse betrayal of their brotherhood with which Oregonians charge all pilgrims from the golden south. Worse yet, I suffer the stigma affixed to anyone from the extreme reach of the state, where the wealth of sunshine is looked upon as the hedonist's blight. I make no pretense of disowning any of it. My place in the historical backwash rests assured.

To claim I moved for the fishing would be stretching it. After ten years of furiously treading water, my wife felt the Southland undertow get the best of her. Raised in the tides, I'd learned to wade cautiously, and I was slow to recognize the symptoms as she went in over her head. They don't hand out survival manuals. The beaches lie littered with twisted dreams, the flotsam and jetsam of a current gone awry, propelled by the promise of sunshine, youth, and permissible greed. You can stand on the shore and hear boys screaming. Nobody yet in the surf is convinced of an abundant universe. Winters, I walked among women sitting in sand, dressed in wool, their arms around their knees, poised as if left there by receding waters. How many tears can one sea hold? I believe children know all of the answers, but by the time my first son was born, I had forgotten how to listen. One day my wife walked down the beach and couldn't find her way back. I stood in the shore break tossing brilliant feathers into pelicans showering down on bait. The second boy arrived, and I looked in his eyes and didn't know who his mother was.

Kay said she needed to be back near family. It was no longer

a question. We put away the Australian immigration papers, and
the life I imagined in Baja suddenly revealed itself as no different
than trying to live on the moon. I still nursed a reckless fantasy
about the Big Lost River near Arco, Idaho, but it made no sense
when all I knew how to do was work for someone else. And it
wasn't as if she were from New Jersey.

We bought a house in Portland for what we sold ours for in
San Diego. A month after we moved in, the worst possible thing
imaginable happened between our twenty-month toddler son
and the young man we'd hired to be his nanny. The fellow got
eight years, and everybody hoped the same sort of thing happened to him while he was there. I don't know why I'm telling
this, but I am. I stayed home with Patch, trying to believe he
would eventually feel safe again in his own home, a prayer I
repeated a thousand times without a whisper in reply.

Come spring, I took a job with a building contractor who
turned out to be an arsonist. Not that he set fire to the houses
he built. Instead, he specialized in burning up employees. Mc
was one of them. He was on his way out, charred and bitter, and
I didn't think a whole lot of him. He mentioned fishing, but a lot
of guys in Oregon do. Six months later, I was right where Mc
had been, sifting through ashes trying to find evidence of my
soul. The new guys didn't think much of me, either.

My first assignment for the arsonist was to ramrod the con-
struction of a show home, the old salary-and-sixty-hours-a-week
gig, holding fire to the feet of underpaid subcontractors. One
afternoon while racing the flames of the deadline, I lost the
inside half of my left index finger to the bite of a Bobcat auger.
That Saturday, Kay announced she had decided not to have an
affair with a guy she had been sharing e-mail with at work. How
come I didn't feel relieved? We started trying to go to church
together as a family, and a few times that summer I drove up the
Clackamas and caught baby trout. I saw God in the guise of a
thousand frogs, the shadows of ghosts of steelhead past.

I was trying desperately to believe. I kept bumping into Mc, and I shared some of my Baja stories with him. He showed me dead fish pictures of his own. Now and then he told me about places to go, but I never quite got around to it. You know how it is when you're alone, ignorant, and afraid.

Finally, with the show home complete and my finger healed, I phoned Mc and he said "Yeah, sure." He met me one Sunday dawn with his drift boat at Wanker's Corner. My life still a firestorm, I'd been on a job site since four, trying to get ready for concrete the next morning. And even after we reached the Deschutes and my heart began to flex, I had difficulty with the light, casting as if through smoke hanging grimly between my eyes.

I never even saw the first fish. It took the fly on the downstream swing, where the little ones sometimes do. But this was something different.

Still, it was another three days before the images began to rhyme. Mc left after our float, and I set up a tent and the next morning tied flies. Shadows appeared, cohering at the margins. I walked the river at dusk, implicating myself within textures that previously had looked flat. I found a narrow slot, a ribbon of the river I could manage in my mind, and each time I visited, I found a little bit better fish.

The last one was good, like the first. But now I wasn't fishing blind. I hiked down to the slot in the midafternoon sun, stretched out on the bank, and sipped a beer. The sage was thick with late-summer sedge, and I poked through a box and found a funky down-wing cinnamon caddis I'd tied ten years before that was perfect. I worked up into the slot, cast by cast, and then shot for the spot where all the others had appeared. The fish came up, pretty as an oil painting, then rode the current out into the deep river proper.

Mc wanted to show me another place, too. For some reason, I expected it to be like somewhere I had been before. The vanity of age astounds me. With so much experience, so many examples, so many waves and rivers and casts and fish, you would think a fellow would come to recognize that each moment is unique. I don't know why that should surprise me anymore. I haven't been anyplace but where I am right now.

The North Fork twists and tumbles, rushes and glides, pools and plummets down the west slope of the Cascades, the perfect trout stream in every way. The watershed, though pockmarked with clear-cuts, remains essentially intact, the integrity of the old-growth biofilter still structurally sound. Fir and cedar fill the sky, and where they topple streamside, the boundary between biological and geological mass becomes obscure, a reduction of nature down to mere elements and hydrology. Root balls as big as one-car garages leave behind gaping pools with access you could ride a bicycle over. Where a tree sinks low enough, the entire stream can change course. Deep in the shadows, beneath layer upon layer of organic matter, the last threshold is finally reached in columns of pure compost as much as six feet deep. At the opposite end of the fecundity scale grow the little calypso orchids that sprout and bloom, only to disappear in days. Sometimes, when you stand within the arc of a crescent-shaped drift, casting in tight to a sheer rock wall dripping water along its entire face, hidden in grasslike uniformity by pendulous maidenhair ferns, it's difficult to know what is stream and what is source, what is feeding and what is fed. Every element exists, braided together pool by pool, the trout but another single thread. Even the fly fisher seems to fit, although I doubt without the angler there would be anything missing.

The first time Mc led me through his favorite beat, I remember thinking, *You can learn everything here there is to know about trout fishing.* The stretch felt as patterned as seashells, the holes laid out one after another, the beginning of each in sight of the last. Though early spring, the stream rushing through the willows, the water ran clear, the freestone streambed visible through shafts of distended light.

We lost flies and caught a few fish that didn't count. I recognized right away the ones that did would be few and far between. But Mc assured me they were there. I was ready to believe. On the deepest crossings, I clung to a wading staff, lifting free of the bottom and bouncing downstream. Mc, fifty pounds heavier and that much taller, kept pointing out spots he had caught fish that now looked more like surf than stream. In camp that night, we fell into talk about chutes and ladders, a cryptic metaphor that had as much to do with one's intermittent progress as an angler as it did the structure of the North Fork, with its sequence of pools, riffles, and rungs of toppled trees. We were drinking too much, fighting off the April chill with a jug of Oregon red. But there was no nonsense to the gratitude I felt for being where I was, having been led there, and sharing it with someone who knew as well as I did that one cast could change your life. And I decided where I wanted to fish the rest of the season.

We returned in two weeks with dogs and my son Patch. Lucy, my new Chesapeake Bay retriever, had mauled Kay while Mc and I were up our first time on the North Fork. I was trying to balance the domestic account. Resigned to such company, Mc brought along Babe, his black Lab, and Daisy, his fiancée's Rottweiler. What this has to do with fishing is best appreciated by those who negotiate such bargains in lieu of a wholesale renunciation of citizenry. My own choices of late had been in favor of a slight declivity toward sanity, following two decades of searching the surf for something that left me face-to-face with the edge. And that little boy with me was the same one I failed and let nightmares envelop his world.

As soon as we hit camp, Lucy crashed through the willows and was swept down a side channel of the river with no apparent escape. While I was fearing for her life, she appeared a hundred yards downstream. She bounded back and pounced again into the current. I could see what we were in for. I got Patch used to riding on my shoulders until I tripped and caught him waist high in front of me, right above the water, after which he refused to cross the stream. Still, the trees had not changed, and the holes remained lined up like designs in royal brocade, and I hoped if I was patient enough, I'd get a chance to insinuate myself into the feel of the fabric at hand.

After another slow morning, we unfurled a river screen I had fashioned out of mosquito netting and two milled cedar sticks. We waded out and rolled rocks. Immediately, everything looked different. Where all along I had been focused on the surface, sighting the occasional March Brown and other spring mysteries, I now stared down at hunks of wriggling meat in the form of handsome stonefly nymphs and, better yet, plump, succulent sculpins the size of Patch's thumbs.

Mc let me know what he thought about my choice of fly, a convulsed Muddler I had dreamed up years ago for Southland bass. He pointed at Lucy, your classic dead-grass Chessie, implying the source of the bug's unruly appearance. But it was not as if I had ever been serious about encountering a sculpin *hatch*.

I drove Mc to the bottom of his beat. He set off with a conventional arsenal of big, black stone nymphs, leaving me with Patch and the dogs. I parked the van at the top of the stretch, near three of the sweetest holes. For once, the dogs kept to themselves. I sat Patch down on a tangle of exposed roots. I shuffled into the water.

Now, you know I am telling all this because I got a good fish. But I don't hope to impress anybody. "You will look upon that which you feel within," I had read someplace recently, and that was the kind of thought I was trying to appropriate, especially when wading out into a picture-perfect pool, my mind conjuring visions of big trout gorging themselves on chunks of helplessly tumbling flesh.

Of course, I had been wading out again and again into just such pools with nothing to show for it. Still, I could see shortly that I was able to get a textbook, end-to-end drift throughout the length of the pool, and I decided with a three-year-old on the bank, I would just stay put for once and keep swimming that big, ugly dog-hair Muddler down through the slot, because if a fish was anyplace, it was here, and I wasn't going to get a better swing anywhere else.

The strange thing is, I killed that fish. I hadn't done that to a trout or its kin since my first steelhead a decade before, immersed then in reasons of vanity no less shallow than this time. There is something to this bloodletting that may well honor a spirit worth recognizing in ourselves, but I don't know that we can indulge this kind of revelation much longer. Patch squatted down next to me as I held the fish tight against the bank and struck it twice with a stone. One eye popped loose, and Patrick squealed. The dogs came running.

But it was an awfully pretty fish, big around as my forearm, with a gentle strip of rose down each side. Back at the van, I climbed out of my waders and held Patch in my arms, letting him run his small hands over the fish's fine scales and broad, spotted tail. Then Mc showed up, cheerily greeting the dogs as they swarmed at his feet.

"So you got one, too!" he announced, producing a mirror image of our own.

I failed to get through to the trauma therapists. The first was a woman, narrow of hip, who never moved past the obvious connections linking my compulsive attitude toward fishing, sex, and a capacity for self-deceit. Later, during a brief fling with anti-depressants, a kindly fellow, bearded and fair, suggested self-esteem exercises that brought to mind adolescence and skin magazines. Neither of them bought the notion that fishing might save my life.

I tried to explain: a big part of the purpose of moving to Oregon was to live somewhere I could fish the fly year-round. The only other sport that had instilled a similar wonder was surfing, but the years spent chasing down good waves around the world had left me jaded, no longer fascinated by the familiar gruel served up along Southland beaches. Age can bring a wicked point of view. And though I had sorted out the mysteries of fly fishing in the surf, the problem of needing to be somewhere else besides home to find good sport remained essentially the same, the outcome of which now seemed the most delicate balance between salvation and an impending sense of doom.

I related my impressions of the winter following Patch's abuse, when I fished with my elder son Speed, in coastal rivers where wild steelhead runs were but stories from the past. Or, better, Speed tagged along, braving the elements, though I did usually choose a relatively benign day, clear and cold, on the chance the water wouldn't be so high. With the fly and hardly a clue as to the true nature of the fish, I contended I was essentially dreaming, exploring new country and water and chalking up days to experience. I didn't know what effect it had on Speed, all this driving and walking and casting called fishing, but for me, there was a grim sense of holding on, trying to make recognizable something that for the life of me I couldn't understand. I fished in rhythms of the simpleton or madman in places where there were no fish, in rivers where the steelhead were lost. But I believed it impossible the fish were truly gone, their spirit dead. Some perfect thread remained embroidered in each river, and I sought it out, cast after cast, searching the heavy water with my big surf rod and bold, indelicate flies, trying to connect with that hidden spirit, be one with it and whole.

I told about the day on the Trask we came upon a dozen rotting salmon carcasses, with the body of a dog directly above them at the high-water mark in the trees. That same morning, in a turnout above the river, we discovered a bear skin discarded down the embankment. I was a stranger that winter to the place I was raising my sons. I had nothing to show Speed I knew anything about. In the mirror as we drove over the coast range back to the city, I watched him sleep, remembering how I used to drift off listening to the engine, daydreaming about waves I had played in all day. Their faces at rest can be so inscrutable: how are we to know anything that haunts their hearts? For once, the passion for fishing seemed more about ideas than anything else: more about protecting than catching fish, more about protecting rivers and streams, protecting the home. The fly that winter kept me safely in the water when all around me I sensed a world more dangerous than I had ever imagined. I believed in a fish I never saw, an entire sport without evidence of participants. The fly and Speed linked me to some perfect truth I was never going to know. But it was reason, I explained, to keep casting.

I made it a year with the slash-and-burn contractor. Then Mc and I decided to partner up and try to make a living between fishing trips. We took a framing job, a two-story fourplex in the heart of Portland. I was really too old for this kind of thing. But it fit perfectly into the schedule, the completion date right before a Father's Day weekend on the North Fork.

Spring rains began holding us up. We had counted on that, but after stacking the roof, we got into one of those wet spells when everything takes longer than planned. There's only so much pickup you can do on a job that size. Finally, one morning, the sky lifted, and after coffee, I hopped up on the top plate to hang fascia.

The building was square, the fascia, affixed to the rafter tails, just a two-by-four. It was an extra on the job, and I had bid it out at half a day for two guys. I had been back walking plate for a month now, so it was nothing to be up there on my own. By lunchtime, I was three-quarters of the way around the building, counting the money with my mind's eye on a new pair of waders.

The evening before, Mc and I had sat down with beers and planned out the entire summer. This job here, that job there. Mc was going to Colorado in September to get married. He had a salmon trip set to Canada with his dad in July. I had decided I wanted to see the North Fork every month of the season. There were jobs we had to refuse. Finally, we got everything to mesh, an honest blend of work and sport without the bullshit of running around stomping out another man's fires.

I was down to two sticks of fascia. Mc, who hates working up high, hollered up and said I could have all the money. I was doing all the work, and it was extra anyway. I could see myself in a pair of fancy lightweight waders, hopping along the North Fork in summer, cool as a warbler, instead of wilting inside my heavy rubber Seal-Dris. Liquid shadows rippled along the length of my leader, the big hopper twisting gaily through tiny eddies, dancing down the mystery slot, gentle as hope, the impeccable blemish on the trout's pure window into spirit's very . . .

Then I was on the ground. I remember thinking, *I am very, very lucky.* I moved, just enough to know that I could, then I lay there and waited for help. I figured if someone would just come massage the muscles in my lower back, I would be okay, and if not that weekend, certainly by the next, I could join Mc on the stream. As I said, I was feeling lucky.

There's a pool on the North Fork between the Forest Service campground and the upper bridge that bends through a hundred yards of perpetual shade, a deep, dark stretch speckled with little trout that rise freely to the fly. I call it Last Chance, The Glory Hole, or Patch's, depending on my mood. I have to believe there is more than one big fish in there. On the other hand, anything even ten inches means you've initiated yourself into the hierarchy. Not that size is the end-all criterion for anything that matters. But you do hope to find one.

I get Patch to stand off to one side so that he doesn't hook me at the end of his Zebco. He is rigged up with a bobber, three feet of leader, and a fly—not one of my best. We are down near the tailout, on a broad band of sand and gravel, that perfect balance sheet accounting for the cyclical rise and fall of the river. In front of us, where the grain size decreases, finally diminishing to silt, the calm, clear water is alive with yearling trout.

Patch lobs the little bobber to the far side of stream, a nice piece of work for a three-year-old. He's been known to call out "Beautiful cast!" But this time, he's content I am watching, the two of us intent on the drift of the fly. First one, then another fish hits it, until the fly is under water and Patch begins to reel in. Yet the fly returns empty, the bobber bouncing noisily over the streamside cobble.

"No fish," announces Patch, as would a passerby offer a greeting. Convinced already that such results are expected, if not also appropriate, he is approaching most everything I've learned about the sport. Free from hope, he lifts another graceful arc toward the far bank.

He tried to tell us. For a week, maybe more, Patch screamed each morning the nanny arrived. We assigned it the label of "a stage," the final catchall for the mysteries faced parenting. I do believe Patch's purpose here is to save us. One night, we noticed bruising over half of his bottom. Kay immediately phoned the nanny, who said Patch had slipped on a mopped floor. I thought maybe Patch had fallen in the gravel under the swing set. Realities beyond imagination are hardest to perceive.

I guess it was like lifting the river screen from the North Fork, those big sculpins and stone nymphs rising into view, opening my mind. I went to change Patch's diaper one evening shortly after the nanny left to catch his bus and his penis was horribly swollen, the scrotum discolored and bruised. It seems so obvious now, but we still couldn't see it. We did have sense enough to take Patch directly to the doctor. He told us the nature of the problem.

I move up the pool, leaving Patch behind while reaching the line farther and farther upstream. I've got a little gray nymph on, my Ugly Emerger, fished just out of sight on a long, greased leader such that there's no easy way to know precisely what is going on. Like the sky on a Russell Chatham canvas, the shade on the water is impossibly full, containing everything there is. I throw a soft, fat loop that disappears before it opens, and then I find the end of the fly line and try immediately to sort out what's happening twelve feet away—as if watching the heroine read the fateful letter while her lover gets mugged offstage.

I come up tight on just a little something. I didn't expect anything else. Does it matter if you do? Backpedaling, I wade downstream to Patch, calling ahead I've got something to show him. I take his rod and give him mine, steadying it while he gets the reel spinning, his left hand groping for a balance point each time I start to let go. The long rod stands practically at rest. It's unclear whether Patch has any concept at all of the line passing through the distant tip, his attention focused instead on the movements of reel and hand. Then, suddenly, the little trout is in the air, dangling above the edge of the shade, brilliant in the same sunlight absorbed by Patch's smile.

"It's a fish," he says, as if until that moment this was all about something else.

I catch a swing of the leader and slip the fish from the fly and hold it down in the water. Patch likes to touch them. There is wonder in his hands, the eyes of discovery in the caress of his small fingers. He struggles with fear, too: he recoils abruptly when the tiny trout tries to escape, and I let it go rather than risk squeezing it. We both laugh, the trout disappearing as if a raindrop in water. Then I point for Patch to look where it might be headed, trying to help him connect the thing that was in my hand with the life within the stream and the dense, liquid shadows.

"Let's go tell Mom!"

I hold the rods in one hand, taking Patch's with the other. He asks me to carry him. I tell him I can't. I take the rod butts and knock them audibly against the front of the brace where a small portion of it shows above my waders, around which my vest can no longer fit. "You know that."

"But your back's getting better."

I hold his small, strong hand and guide him off the stream and into the woods. There's a moment I believe I will bend down and pick him up anyway. It doesn't matter if I can or I can't—he wants me to, so I can. But I can't, and we're just going to have to get used to it.

The Ugly Emerger

We all know the scenario: big, smart trout rolling on the surface, audibly sipping or gulping some invisible fare, the sound of feeding fish punctuating the descent of darkness—that is, the coming of night, not your deepening sense of futility and gloom.

Yet the solution is no mystery, either. Something is emerging, levitating toward the surface in that particularly vulnerable state that entices large trout to feed with obscene confidence. More often than not—especially in that painful moment of twilight's last gleaming—the bugs of note will be some sort of midge pupae, or perhaps little Blue-Winged Olives, or Sulfur miniduns, or the like. Let's just say it's safe to predict these are *small* fellers. Yet at no time of day do you see more large fish burrowing through the surface, exposing themselves with peaceful abandon to the departing light, and at no time of day do you receive more sonic evidence of good trout within casting range conspicuously on the feed.

Slurp, slurp, slurp. . . .

But despite our recognition of these regular, seductive occurrences, very few anglers I know knock them dead. Let's face it: it's a tough go. Low light, minuscule flies, long, frail leaders, delicate casts, and perfect, drag-free drifts, a level of concentration and intense focus on stimuli invisible to the naked eye, more recognizable in fact by some magnanimous sixth sense—all this makes that compressed last hour of fishing for selective trout no picnic. Sometimes I get so frustrated I just back off and watch. Not often, but sometimes.

Because once, perhaps twice an evening, you get it all right.

Or maybe you just get lucky. Or maybe, like the monkey at the typewriter who eventually bangs out a perfectly composed sentence, you randomly put all the pieces in divine alignment—and at that moment, whatever the source of your success, you sense your connection to all manner of things, from the bugs you can't see to the river in which you stand, as a big trout begins to work heavily against the rod.

Of course, it's a problem we never fully unravel. In time, the whole notion of fishing tiny emergers—whether they be nymphs, flymphs, soft hackles, no hackles, stillborns, wingless duns, or sinking dries—the whole notion becomes as much metaphor as actual technique, a commitment of faith that says more about your own emergence as an angler than it does about any stage of an ephemeral insect as prey. Believe me, I'd much rather do something easier. But the simple fact of committing oneself to fly fishing sets in motion a whole range of philosophical attitudes that develop from that first, basic precept. For one, you've eliminated worms, gill nets, and dynamite from your options. Beyond that is a belief in the sublime, a fundamental rightness in a system of ethics that points beyond our own little egos.

But it doesn't happen overnight. Unlike the tiny critter so often mimicked in its brief transitory state of emergence, the transformation from primitive underling to full-blown fly fisherman is a slow and sometimes painful process. Certainly, this is when we're all most vulnerable—not only to the criticisms implied by our actual and frequent failures, but also to an inevitable wavering of faith. Many in fact never get over the deep-seated belief that fishing the fly is actually a *handicap*, that the choice is fundamentally a sacrifice made in the name of sport, the acceptance of a self-imposed challenge in favor of a somehow less effective means of catching fish. Indeed, rarely do you meet a young, emerging fly fisher who feels his or her chances are *better*. Most are guided by some obscure sense of potential grace available to those who submit to scripted limitations, following The Way. Yet what can actually eventually be revealed is a viewpoint of limitless possibilities, a sense of promise that enriches each cast with the same invitation the sky must offer an insect rising through water, its wings beginning to unfold.

You can probably see where I'm going with this: every time I tie on an itty-bitty subsurface bug in anticipation of dusk's final, faint rise, I'm impressed with how far I've come to have faith in what really has little to distinguish itself as a fly from a tuft of navel lint. It says a lot about my belief in the exactitudes of presentation, rather than in patterns. And it says just as much about how far I still have to go to become the fly fisherman I hope one day to be.

But what impresses me most is that this is almost precisely how I started, how I almost always approached big, difficult feeding fish, even without a clue as to why. And so I wonder, sometimes, how much I've really learned at all.

Whatever I did learn at the start was gleaned from a dozen years' trout fishing in tiny streams in California's southern Sierra Nevada, where our "method" was a distillation of any and all fine points, down to your basic dapping technique. What that meant was a store-bought size 16 or 18 Mosquito tied to a rod's length of light leader, the whole of which was presented commando-style through brush and thickets, over boulders and fallen trees. Clella Snider, who was brilliant at it, called it "dingle fishing." My dad's buddy Bill's wife, she'd stay back at camp dealing with kids and breakfast, only to sidle out as the sun warmed the air and bugs began to show, soon to return with her limit. Of course, we did also cast. But it was clear such efforts were mainly about displaying developing rod-handling skills and losing flies—not about catching fish. Occasionally, in the face of a particularly unresponsive trout, we might also slip a salmon egg onto the fly.

And like a lot of other unfortunate angling souls, I spent time now and then fishing for woeful, mass-produced trout in Southland reservoirs—which was just too moribund for words.

Still, by the time I'd attained a semblance of adulthood, I considered myself a true fly fisherman, fairly handy with a rod and able to distinguish an Adams from a Royal Coachman—no small achievement for a child of the freeway suburbs and a pronounced Mediterranean clime. Following college, I had an opportunity to help build a log cabin in Idaho, which I accepted, visions of trout usurping my usual infatuation with shapely sunspeckled waves. This would have also been about the time I started growing pot for personal use, a pastime that got entirely out of hand. So I was subject in those days to a lot of, shall we say, visions. Nevertheless, the cabin site was in verifiable trout country, looking out at the back side of the Tetons above Driggs, and occasionally I ventured out and found fish, not wholly unlike those I knew from the High Sierra.

Then Peter arrived. At the time, he wasn't what I would call a really close friend, though obviously when a guy drives a thousand miles to go fishing with you, there's something there. He had just returned from Australia, having invested his share of the neighborhood pot harvest in the exquisite waves at Queensland's Kirra Point, and I think it fair to say Peter was, at the time, just as impressionable as I was, the good grass we had around being what it was. Yet we had been fishing together in the surf a couple of seasons, known each other from the beach and building surfboards, and had shared student/surfer housing longer than that. So it wasn't as if we had never *talked* about trout. On the other hand, our budding friendship had taken root more through literature than sport, the spirit of such novels as *The Naked and the Dead*, *Sometimes a Great Notion*, and *Gravity's Rainbow* providing the perfect counterpoise for whiffs of flight and fancy we were known to suffer while gazing lustfully out at waves.

Anyway, Peter showed up—and the intensity of the fishing immediately jumped a notch. Peter already knew how to tie flies, and he graciously allowed me to pick through his, a practice I indulged in for years and never fully appreciated until I began tying my own. This would also be the first time I ever heard about tapered leaders. As I said, up to this point, I hadn't learned much of anything about trout fishing.

We were a curious pair, Peter and I. All my fly fishing had been hand-me-down, field-tested, trial-and-error, hunt-and-dink guerrilla tactics. Peter had learned by *reading* about it. If he hadn't, he would have had nothing to go on: remarkably, he came from a family in which his father didn't fish. There had been some summer camp in the Trinity Alps at which he had been exposed to trout. But that was pretty much it—other than what he gathered out of books and outdoor magazines and eventually sorted out on dinky creeks of his own.

I didn't even know that people wrote about fly fishing— except Hemingway, and that never seemed remotely like anything I had ever done. Except lately, when the *tinto* came out along the stream.

The first evening, we wandered down to an access spot along the Teton River and killed a pair of whitefish. Our host, whose cabin I had been helping with, could hardly believe his eyes. He didn't exactly hold his nose, but he made it clear to us *he* never brought such fish home. We ate them and discovered why. Of course, we soon did catch trout. And I remember one particular rainbow, your classic foot-long, one-pound fish in a tight, fast riffle beneath the willows, where only the quick and strong survive, the sort of trout that just *slams* the fly and then seems entirely out of proportion to the water, your excitement, and its eventual diminutive size. But a lot of things seemed out of proportion back then.

In August, we drove up to Yellowstone. The park was so crowded we left our cars at the campground and hitchhiked around, taking in the usual tourist sights without any real notions about fishing. Then we saw the trout under Fishing Bridge. That afternoon, we tossed grasshoppers by hand into the Firehole, bringing fish to the surface as if in a dream.

A ranger told us about Pelican Creek. We hiked in and discovered that the reason the roads were so crowded was because nobody was on the trails. An elderly couple was just leaving the stream, the only other people for miles of classic oxbow meadow in either direction. We asked them how they had done. You could still keep fish back then in the park, and when they opened their creel, I remember thinking I would never catch such big trout in all my life.

At the first pool, I saw one. Its wake unfolded bank to bank. I dug through my fly box and tied on the smallest thing I had. Later, when Peter and I rejoined upstream, I showed him evidence of the kind that can ruin your life.

"Goddamn, you got one," he said.

Then Peter got them, too. The stream was low and clear, victim of the drought the West had suffered two years running. We fished the longest, lightest tippets we dared, reveling in the newfound distances afforded by unobstructed backcasts. "This is just how it's supposed to be!" we both announced—as if up to now there had been some promise that fly fishing had failed to keep.

Still, it was hard enough that we usually didn't get it right. In fact, we were so new to this level of sport that when we did catch fish, we believed it meant we had done *everything* right. We learned to grease our leaders to within an inch or two of the fly, then soak the dark speck in spit so that it hung directly in the surface film, or a fraction of an inch below. The take, sometimes impossibly faint, was as sweet as tube riding when you connected.

But what we didn't know was how much we really didn't know. Not only were we nearly clueless about almost everything you *could* do right, we were equally ignorant of the fact that doing "everything right" was not necessarily what the sport was all about: that by its very nature, fly fishing might be about what's *out* of our control, not what's in it; that the spirit of fly fishing may well be the very same spirit that moves or doesn't move the fish to the fly, so that what you are fishing for is beyond anything you can catch, but merely the echo of some indefatigable will, revealed in bits and pieces along the water's streamy edge.

Now because this is a chronicle about becoming a fly fisherman—and all the shadows that followed me along—I want to speak, just for the record, about the last time I ever used spinning gear.

This is a touchy subject: my father, for one, loves the stuff. I also have been known to wade out into heavy surf and heave a big, chrome spoon at the end of a long jigging rod and conventional-wind Penn Jigmaster, a transgression in certain angling circles as serious in these temperate times as a fondness for ninety-proof whisky.

And there is also a woman involved, not the one who became my wife and the mother of my two sons. So you can understand if I've a sense that I need to tread lightly.

I drove with Miss B from San Francisco to Bishop by way of Tioga Pass, introducing her to a scale of mountain range that the string of volcanoes called the Cascades can never really approach. Miss B was originally from Seattle. Let's leave it at that. We met Peter and another pal from La Jolla at the Foster Freeze, and then we caravanned to the North Lake trailhead and packed over Piute Pass into Humphreys Basin. I'm making this sound easier than it is. But I had been living in the city longer than a man of my temperament should, and I was eager to get on the water, any water, and, you know, *fish*.

Miss B did keep up. And for awhile she tried her hand at sport—although it was Peter who took the time to do more than thrust a rod at her, point at the water, and tell her to go to it. I still feel bad about this. Poetically, on our second night above timberline, I reached into Miss B's pack for toothpaste, only to discover while brushing that instead of Crest, I had grabbed the Nivea Skin Creme.

We were up at golden trout altitudes, fishing in a milieu of sun-shot and wind-beaten granite that belies most traditional trout techniques. Falling back on old habits (I almost wrote "bad"), I was spin-casting a fly and bobber, or occasionally even a little Super Duper. There was one tiny feeder creek near our base camp that I did fly fish properly, the brilliant six-inch and seven-inch fish rushing like flames to the fly. But mostly I was content to circle lake after lake, casting and retrieving, casting and retrieving, picking up the random decent fish in a manner of dull-witted, spurious hoodwinking that has its own tenor as sport.

Meanwhile, Peter was mindfully approaching the true game at hand. He killed a couple fish and inspected their stomach contents, a procedure once as foreign to me as ending a fish's life by rapping it over the head, rather than allowing it to suffocate and simply perish. Inside each fish was a plug of little black morsels, as if you had made a cigarette-sized sausage filled with coffee grounds. Closer inspection revealed wads of ants, remarkable in the sheer numbers it took to create them. Later, Peter pointed out ants scurrying atop the granite boulders surrounding at least three sides of every lake we fished, and when the wind blew, he noticed ants sprinkling the water.

So did the trout. Peter was fishing the same little dark thing we'd relied on in Yellowstone, casting to cruising feeders he could see, or just hanging it out there until he got hit. Pretty soon I began to feel coarse. It wasn't that Peter was doing any better than I was: he wasn't catching more fish, or bigger ones. (Although they might have been *a little* bigger.) But there was just so much more grace involved—from the cast to the strike, from the fight to the landing. Not to mention the *thought* that went into each fish. And I guess what really got me was I could see Peter was having more fun.

Toward the end of the trip, we returned to a lake where we had caught our largest fish, some pushing a solid foot, which was still our notion of an awfully decent trout. Miss B stayed back at camp, foretelling the outcome of our relationship, and I left my spinning gear there, too—the last time I had any along anywhere when I had to decide whether to use it. The lake was nestled into high, steep slopes of dislodged boulders, with nothing recognizable as plant life for as far as the eye could see. We clambered around to the upwind side of the lake, where sharp gusts pulsed down the mountain and showed as surface chop on the water, and we kited out long casts or took potshots into the glassy slicks tucked in tight against the granite. The fish showed where they should, some of them sighting the fly from a dozen feet away. I read poetry, but it's never this sweet. Later, during a lull, we heard a strange *whooshing* noise descending on us, then suddenly at our rod tips appeared a peregrine on the tail of a swift or swallow. It missed—but for Peter and me, that wasn't the point.

"Did you see what I saw?"

So how do you tie this little emerger I've been using as my ace in the hole since the beginning of time? A fair question, but from what I know to date, the answer is worth a wooden nickel. Granted, I do grow excited sometimes, trying to piece together the right colors and proportions, the proper profile and latest materials. But I'll be frank and tell you I think it's mostly hype. I mean, the *concept* of the fly is sound, and over the years, I've hooked by far the largest percentage of my truly big trout on what looks like little more than a beauty mark on the fish's lip. I like to *believe* it matters whether or not I tail these flies, whether they're ribbed or weighted or tied to float upside down. I also trouble myself about what material to employ in the underdeveloped wing pad, or how long to make the stillborn's trailing nymph husk. Then I get a magazine in the mail and see a new pattern and say to myself *That's it!* and rush downstairs to the basement office vise to start twisting.

And then, when I'm on the water, I see something that is really going to make a difference, and in camp that evening or in the aroma of morning coffee, I tie up another couple little goodies, this one with just enough that, that one with just enough this.

But I know I already have every such fly I need. From CDC Emergers to Serendipities, from tiny *Baetis* nymphs to Swannundaze Midges, from Micro Pheasant Tails to Brassies to Crossbred Chronomid Scuds, my arsenal is sufficiently stocked with the best of the best. And the no-names—which outnumber the others ten to one—take care of the rest.

I just don't think it's that important—once you decide to go tiny right *in* the surface—whether your bug is fashioned out of peacock herl or Antron or kinky Betts's Z-lon. Mysteries are never revealed in a gospel of patterns and techniques. The best answer may well be the one you don't know. That little emerger is the means, not the end. The other good news might be that you are, too.

So this is me in the little town of McCloud in, say, 1980—give or take a year. I've got one of the family split-cane rods with me, along with my pack and journals. I've been on the road the past four or five years, half of them overseas, standing tall in the face of questions about my future and surfing. It's the last Saturday of April, Opening Day, and the night before I arrived by Greyhound in Shasta City and called a cab rather than brave the heavy rain, luxuriating in the final twenty miles, despite the bite out of my already perilously diminished stake.

The rain turns to snow overnight, and outside my window is

a postcard of Mount Shasta, brilliant in the morning sun. I don't deserve this, but who else does? I've got a clean room with a bed and a desk, toilet down the hall, paid in full for a month, and I pore over maps until I can't stand it anymore, giving in at last to longing looks at my disassembled gear.

There is a profound surrender to spirit in exploring new waters without means of transportation—unless of course you can afford a stay at the Caddis Banquet Riverside Lodge, which naturally relegates the kind of thing I'm talking about to a moot point. Each day, I'd head off out of town in the general direction of the river, either east, along the state highway toward the falls and upper sections, or south, toward the dam and access to the then recently designated blue-ribbon catch-and-release water. Little streams intersect both routes. Don't expect me to remember names. Once on the road, I'd wave my thumb at passing vehicles, relying more on the display of my rod case. I got rides from all sorts, from families on vacation to fathers looking for work, from moms doing grocery shopping to your hard-core bucket brigaders. They all knew something about the trout fishing. None of them agreed how to go about it.

I don't recall any really outrageous fish that spell. There was a short stretch of pocket water just above the falls that was usually good for a rowdy take or two, and in the big pools below each fall I could pretty well count on a number of the stocked browns, oftentimes taken in full view of a bait or metal caster. The blue-ribbon water was tough, no question about it, and by the end of the month, the rattlesnakes were moving, which made you feel like you definitely earned each fish. But mostly I ended up on small, out-of-the-way water, by choice or chance, I don't know which. And like a lot of anglers fishing alone, that's where I had the most fun, my little emergers and tiny dries producing fish after fish in the heart of the intimate rise.

I took what came and was happy for it. I saw myself as a fly fisherman, the genuine article, untroubled by my lack of direc-

tion or expertise. The goal, like my life, was essentially pointless—other than living on the water, flies in the film, now and
then pricking a sparkling trout.

Shortly before my money ran out, though, I met a sportsman
just back from a thirsty petroleum project in Saudi Arabia. Flush
with cash and stateside liberties, he had loaded the shallow
trunk of a brand-new Triumph with lord knows how much
money's worth of fly gear, driving north from San Francisco and
looking to nail himself some good trout. The first night, after fishing, he came by with a case of Hamm's to recite "Ode to the
Ocean," a heartfelt verse he admitted credit for only after I com-
plimented his serious, albeit gently slurred rendition. Strangely, I
suddenly became the man in the know, the guy who supposedly
knew the ropes and the water, the guide with the situation
under control. It was as if I were being courted, or insinuated
into a scheme, and at that moment things all began to change.

I fished with this fellow for days, making less happen than
had happened by itself when I was on my own. He was a type,
your basic mid-thirties ex-Green Beret with ballsy good looks
and thinning, sun-bleached hair. Drinking or not, he told a good
story, said he used to manage an alligator farm somewhere in
Central America, and that first weekend he even attended the
local community dance—chaperoned, no less—trying to pick up
the checker he had met at the McCloud grocery store. There was
also a lot of talk about cocaine, although fortunately his pragmatic Arkansas upbringing kept that kind of thing pretty much
in check unless he was clearly on the heels of a hot number. We
raced about like retrievers casting for a scent, over to the
Sacramento and across to the Pit and the Fall. We caught small,
stupid trout, and little else.

There was a lesson here, if I could pay attention. The harder
this guy tried, the worse things turned. Back on my local beat
one day, the guy took a terrific fall down into the pocket-water
canyon, sliding fifty yards headfirst on his stomach, somehow

without breaking rod or limb. Later, over on the Sacramento, he tried a reckless cast in a right-hand wind and buried a big Deer Hair Caddis in his ear.

Finally we up and left McCloud, tying my pack onto the trunk rack and heading for the valley. We stopped at his aunt's double-wide in Redding and drank beer, talking about the small-mouth bass fishing in Lake Shasta, the two of them denigrating it in comparison with Razorback sport. Then we rode I-5 down to the East Bay, Walnut Creek or the like, our descent punctuated by frequent bar stops and ill-received propositions.

It turned out there was a pending job interview with another big petro corporation overseas. I remember driving up and down a generic suburb boulevard searching unsuccessfully for a vacant motel room, the guy growing more and more upset. "I'm a fucking materials superintendent!" he shouted at one point.

We ended up in a place where a couple of his Saudi work buddies were staying, also awaiting job interviews. That evening, I was approached with accusations regarding cash under some-body's pillow. This wasn't about fishing anymore, and I knew it. Something was at work in my life right then, and it wasn't doing me a lot of good or teaching me a thing about how or why a fish might take a fly. In the morning, I asked to be dropped off at the nearest Greyhound station, heading north for no more reason, once again, than for the hell of it.

But this time that didn't work, either. Emergence complete, flight loomed as perilous as love. Down to my last dollar, I took a job driving tractor on a lily farm north of Eureka. I caught one fish that summer, a heartbreakingly beautiful rainbow up on Redwood Creek, which I stashed overnight in a rain gutter because I was too tired to eat and the room I was renting was without a refrigerator. Gritty and lonely, I spent weekends in the public library, discovering Roderick Haig-Brown, Russell Chatham, Thomas McGuane. I began to entertain notions of fly fishing for fish other than trout, especially in the margins of the surf. So much about trout fishing suddenly seemed studied, prescript, refined. I loved the idea of big beaches, big water, and big fish. And I loved the idea of big flies—with surfboards back in camp, should *that* game unfold.

I took my hard-earned savings down to the local Long's Drugs, stocked in those parts as well as any sporting-goods shop. I remember being unable to decide which new fly line to purchase, literally weighing each choice in my hands. Weight Forward Fast Sink? Intermediate Saltwater Rocket Taper? Super Hi-Speed Hi-D *Shooting Head*? Finally I pocketed one and went and paid for another.

I was grabbed outside the store and steered into a cop car. I began whimpering like a scolded three-year-old. This wasn't how it was supposed to be. The hardass at the station wanted to know what the fuck I was doing in his town anyway. When I told him where I had been working, he shook his head and said, "Bulb picker." He might just as well have said "Shit sucker."

I spent a week composing a letter feebly pleading my case. At the courthouse on the appointed day there was no record of my name: a complaint hadn't been filed, charges had not been pressed. I walked out onto the street, in the summer North Coast fog, and headed directly to the drugstore and bought and paid for that second fly line. I rode the bus south that day, resting overnight at Miss B's sister's place in San Francisco. In a week I was in Baja, and not long after that catching fish in the surf on flies. I sensed a direction in all of this, and that maybe even the direction was good. It did seem worth the effort to find out. The way things went with Miss B's sister that night may or may not have proved me right.

Beneath the Borderlands
FROM SEPIC'S JOURNALS

No hay peor lucha que la que no se hace.
There's no worse struggle than one that never begins.
—Folk wisdom of Mexico

*T*he first thing I'm always asked about are the stories. You know the ones I mean. Guy breaks down below Tijuana . . . *federales* . . . "I wasn't doing anything wrong!" . . . Dope/booze/women/children/dogs—take your pick . . . "No money, no go-ee" . . . slashed tires . . . *banditos* . . . jail hell . . . the donkey and the . . . It's a marvelous litany of the horrors and evils that have long befallen innocent travelers in a strange, foreign land. The most astonishing fact is that anyone has ever returned to tell the tale. Because they're all true—every last one of them. As the great Lopez said, waving his arm toward a very different kind of surf for the ABC *Wide World of Sports* camera: "It's the *Banzai* Pipeline: guys die out here all the time."

In the summer of 1961, my father and his buddy Bill Snider decided it was time to venture farther south. Angel's Camp, today the Las Salinas exit on the Tijuana-to-Ensenada toll road, had declined even then beyond hope, exhibiting a tendency in favor of the sort of morbid gringo indiscretion for which that particular stretch of coastline would soon gain infamy. Lobster aficionados both, my father and his best friend and diving pal steered their two young families down the final sixty miles of pavement below Ensenada, searching for yet another remote Baja beach partitioned off by rocks "crawling with bugs" where kids of all ages could run safe and free.

For a full decade, we capered in the isolated dunes and chilly

surf alongside Punta Cabras, also known as K-181 in that innocent manner of identifying beach turnoffs by their distance
beneath the border. *Longosta* notwithstanding, our sport was
restrained by the cold sea and foggy summer winds, a pronounced temperament produced by the harmonics of currents
between Punta Banda, near Ensenada, and Punta Baja, some forty
miles south of San Quintin. Yet in the histories of our families,
these were sovereign times: childhoods were breached, pubes-
cence ascertained, and, presumably, menstruations commenced.
And I do remember, with a sort of beguiling fatalism, the one trip
on which we shared our reverie with other gringos, a crew of
young California surfing archetypes, virile hedons who disem-
barked, boards and all, from a bald-tired nine-passenger family
station wagon, then proceeded to engage in all manner of gregar-
ious merriment, not the least of which involved dangerous
explosives launched at a kite flown with a casting rod, as well as
the countless hours spent skimming the horizon on waves, suddenly transfigured into almost angelic shapes.

I do believe that Bonnie Snider, Bill's eldest, would also
remember one of those fellows, or at least the feel of his hand in
hers as they departed one afternoon down the windswept sand.

It was the lure of my own surfing fantasies that eventually
spirited me into the heart of deepest Baja. On a trip to the mainland, I met a pair of "older" guys—at that time any surfer over
twenty-five—who had just descended the length of the peninsula on the recently opened paved highway before taking the
ferry from La Paz. To me, their talk of endless shorelines, empty
vistas, and crackling desert barrels was nothing less than a
promise of salvation. I was on my own long, wavy road at that
juncture, headed for El Salvador, Costa Rica, and all edges of the
night, yet I understood that I was eventually to return to my
degraded Southland shores. I knew Baja would serve as a frequent retreat. And as these things happen in our lives, those
breaking, spiraling waves I had imagined would one day save me,

actually did. But rather than on a surfboard—although that was certainly part of it—grace came while struggling for footholds dancing chest-deep in that very surf, casting big, bright flies into big, bright fish rushing shoreward with the swing of tides.

It begins with the moon.

Fly fishing in the surf is an invitation to failure, an acceptance of ignorance, a faith in profound revelation. The expanded reach of tides associated with a full or new moon—"spring tides"—offers a framework in which to surrender oneself to the mysterious. At some level, we may recognize these exaggerated lunar tuggings stirring us, along with both predator and prey. I plan every Baja trip—and almost every fishing trip as well—around the dark of the moon. I like to think the lack of light also inhibits nightly feeding. And as these things work, you get the all-important push toward high tide precisely when it counts most—once in the morning, once in the eve.

Moon, tides, wind, current, sun—these are all ingredients of the surf, a complex mixture of enigmatic forces into which we can hope at best to intuit some order. Watch a wave break, notice where a good surfer rides: the vibrant periphery between foamy white water and surface blues or greens describes with accuracy the contours and patterns below. Holes, pockets, reefs, ridges, channels—where are the fish going to lie? The surf is a natural translation for fly fishers keyed to the dynamics of rivers and streams. Expand that notion, the image, your mind. . . . The big trout is in the slot. Swing the fly right to him.

Maybe you like to fish bass—you know, *structure*. So what's that all about? What's happening? Drift a deep-sunk fly along the ledge, behind the reef, over the kelp. Think about a pinball in slow motion and guide the fly from obstacle to obstacle, hollow to hollow. This isn't always pretty. If you don't stop the fish right *now*, he's back home, and you're beat. Maybe you should have tied the leader tight to the end of a long, stout cane pole.

Those big spring tides, packaged with dramatic lows, also provide an opportunity to wander through the very terrain you'll be fishing over a few hours later. Watch the water recede. Follow the course of the flood pushed by the intervals of waves. The fly and the fly line are the needle and thread with which you will trace your memory of this tapestry of currents. I'm forever thinking about these slots and channels in the surf. In my mind's eye, the fly is swimming through a vein, an artery, a stream of clear water, a path of gathered energy, a game trail through the jumbled woods.

It's always a guess: what *else* is new about fly fishing? The essential ingredient is the relatively calm water. There's a look to too much surf that resembles a river that winter steelheaders would recognize as blown. Keep searching. You need at least to *feel* the fish can see your fly.

Beyond that, the thing you really hope to stumble upon is, say, a squadron of pelicans plunging to the surface, or showers of baitfish erupting as if from a submerged, high-pressure fire hose. But, hey, come on. Anybody could tell you that.

Given my Byzantine character and infinite capacity for self-deceit, I believe it dangerous I be the one to direct anybody down a path of this nature. I have enough blood on my hands, so to speak, as it is. Which isn't to abdicate a sense of complicity. I made the choice recently to be helpful where I can, refraining from mercurial attempts to prove my innocence. I just don't want anyone to stand up and say I didn't warn them.

This kind of fishing can ruin you for life. The Baja surf is raw, unpredictable, generous to both empiricism and reckless spontaneity, and virtuously unforgiving of pretension or sporting airs. Let it be known that this is fly fishing that money can't buy. My good buddy Peter once described it as "anarchic, amusing, infinitely entertaining, and at the right price!" He has also appraised it as angling's equivalent to a flying-saucer encounter, which rings true in its own elliptic way.

Nearly all true Baja adventure entails heady road trips—the only means besides luxury yachts and small aircraft by which to experience most of the peninsula shoreline. One of the treasured Baja myths, however, is the need for four-wheel-drive vehicles. My experience is that the guy with the 4WD often gets stuck worse, the delusionary potency of his rig propelling him into situations that the rest of us avoid like sour milk. Stoutness, on the other hand, is to be duly admired. A Baja road can break something in a way that makes merely getting your wheels stuck no worse than morning irregularity. I've always liked the looks of the safari interpretation executed by Mercedes Benz. Meanwhile, back here on earth, the best Baja rig I've owned to date was a '65 GMC pickup, V-6, 305.

Enrique—I'll call him—didn't think that much of it, gesturing with his dark, callused hands. The transmission was too small. He could have told me in Spanish, but maybe he wanted to emphasize the degree of our shortcomings. And anyway, I didn't see how gears of any size would help get us out of this, the very worst kind of slop imaginable, greasy clay cat snot in the pickleweed out by Estero de Coyote, the mangrove near Punta Abreojos.

It's like the feel of falling: *Oh no!* I recall my own swift descent, two stories in the blink of an eye. Getting stuck in Baja is not as dangerous, but still filled with sensations of blunt culpability. At that moment, it's already too late: you were right, you should have taken the other fork. I do believe there's a road to anyplace you want to go in Baja. It's just that the one you choose doesn't always get you there.

Enrique rises after peering under the truck, and I hand him a towel to clean off his hands and the knees of his khaki chinos. He's an old, refined Mexican, owner of a ranch and a Ford pickup with a properly sized transmission. It's not at all clear why he was hanging out around the abandoned *cabanitas* along the lagoon. But as with most Baja locals, whatever Enrique was doing was not so important he couldn't drop it to come inspect someone else's problems.

We get a heavy tow rope affixed between back bumpers. Peter and a new friend, Jakob, a German scientist from the Salk Institute, stand back. Enrique puts his big Ford transmission to work, lifting our truck back up onto the track, from which it immediately slides into the muck on the other side. We try this another half-dozen times, digging on all fours between each attempt. When we finally give up, Enrique is more than just a little disappointed in his truck.

The part I like most about these days is the happy endings. The part I don't like is the hard work, the grime, and, naturally, losing valuable fishing time. Enrique drives me into town at Abreojos, where we locate a fellow with a full-sized Bronco. We drive back to my truck, break the rope twice, then return to town for proper equipment: a chain, Hi-Lift jack, and a couple dozen empty ready-mix concrete sacks for traction. Enrique refrains from making this second trip, motioning with his hand the nature of the washboard road then pointing at his lower back. When my truck does finally come out, throwing concrete sacks every which way, it leaves a furrow as deep as a sewer-line trench.

I give the Bronco owner and Enrique a twenty-dollar bill each. We all agree what matters most is getting the job done. Driving back to camp, I remark to Peter and Jakob that it sure feels good not to have had to leave the truck behind. And *tomorrow* we'll knock them dead. We head into the setting sun, squinting hard atop the rises.

If a Baja trip were all about catching fish, even the finial graces of catching surf fish on the fly, I would be hard put to argue for the effort required to explore these desolate reaches.

Time, too, seems a factor out of proportion, pressing the accept-able margins for sport, although if time is money, knowing the dollar-per-fish ratio now commonly spent on trout makes the equations in Baja appear prudently more balanced. Still, it would seem to me that fishing itself has come to mean something other than what can be justified in any sort of budgetary reckoning, whether the medium of exchange be time, effort, money, *or* social responsibilities. Naturally, having reached the age of forty, I'm to be excused for making this sort of observation.

Here's another kind of Baja trip, presented to illustrate the elaborate dimensions in which I've come to frame the relatively simple portrait of hooking a fish in the surf on a fly. Along this time are Kay, her mother, and my then week-from-one-year-old son Speed. After three days on a Pacific beach without seeing a single other human being—gringo *or* local—Speed's grand-mother is ready to jump ship when we reach the cosmopolitan gaiety of gulf-side Santa Rosalia. "Don't worry," I assure her. "This next spot is *just like Hawaii.*"

Yet when we finally descend from the washboard, swinging down onto the beach beneath the cliffs at Bahia de Muertos—Dead Man's Bay—I note with a certain lassitude that the scene is not nearly as alluring as it had seemed when arriving in the company of more sanguinary travelers. The turkey vultures scattered about in attitudes of repose around the grave markers may have something to do with it. Still, the sea is as bright blue as any, the air temperature a benign notch or two below triple figures, feel-ing even cooler due to the crackling lack of humidity. "Just like Hawaii!" I repeat, drawing Coronas off the block of ice that seems in four hours already to have shrunk in half.

This will be a visit during which I catch cabrilla and pargo, countless ladyfish, small jacks, and one tiny rooster. It's May, late spring, perhaps the slowest season in Baja, though not so bereft of sport that the engagement of an Oregon mother-in-law—

seduced by the promise of sun—to share baby-sitting duties should be denied. I have stooped lower. This will also be where Speed, troubled by fiery cobblestones, abruptly stands and begins walking. Another incident of note is the afternoon I arrive back in camp and suffer the explicit retelling of how the shade canopy blew down in the breeze, a set of circumstances that "could have killed somebody." It is also made clear to me that such things would not possibly happen in Hawaii.

The day before leaving, I fish on into evening, only to return to camp to discover we've been visited by a pair of local fellows, now parked a respectful distance away, heartbreaking Latino music blaring from speakers set atop their little import's roof. Kay and her mother are visibly shaken. Despite repeated admonitions that the fishing is below par—"Fishing no good!"—Kay has been unable to persuade the pair to leave. I stroll over to chat. Their intent never does become precisely clear, beyond the logical fact that this is the end of the road to the beach. Later, we go around to the trunk, opened to reveal an oversized ice chest. Inside lies the biggest pargo by far I have ever seen, twenty-five, maybe thirty pounds, caught on a handline that looks to test out at around a hundred pounds—exactly the gear necessary to subdue this sort of monster around reefs and rocks, where I've lost countless flies this trip, except to the bantam pargo of two and three pounds that I've managed to stop with my 12-pound tippets. I holler for the gals and Speed to come look.

Or this . . . the day with Peter and my father when up and down the beach we were witnesses to spurts of bait, nothing consistent or concentrated enough to allow us to get on top of them, but evidence of big fish roving, nonetheless, out there and cruising, and as soon as the sun dropped, we were most certainly going to nail them. This went on all through the afternoon. We tied flies, brewed coffee, watched the random spray of silver frenzy, and gabbled on and on about what it was going to be like when one of those darlings sidled up—oh my!—to that sweet, sweet streamer.

I was in full stride along the beach the moment the shadow touched the water. I knew a slot down a ways where things always seemed to, you know, *happen*. Up ahead in the sunlight, the bait continued to show—then, suddenly, I had this painful sensation that where I was wasn't where the fish were anymore. I started to trot, trying to catch up with what was already gone, the lemon taste of despair spreading through my mouth. I don't take this kind of thing very well. As I reached the end of the beach, the excitement draining out of me, I remembered a phrase from a McGuane essay, something about the whole factory shutting down. I repeated the phrase out loud—"the whole goddamn factory shut down!"—kicking sand in the pettiest fashion, knowing just how silly I must look as I did it again and again, feeling a lot as if the sand were me. Who can I blame for this, lifting wan casts from an empty sea?

Now, there's another kind of moment in Baja I want to mention, an idiosyncrasy in the private itinerary I've shaped around all the good fishing. Going north, coming home, I like to stop and spend the night in the high, twisted desert between Guerrero Negro and San Quintin. It's either that, or you're back up in the borderlands, and you might as well push on home.

I don't think it matters much where you stop. You want to get off the highway, safely out of sight, and, more important, out of earshot from the diesel traffic. Yet even more than that, you'll be spreading your bedroll in a place that's wild and not much else, a place too harsh for anyone to tame, a place where everything you look at is how it's always been, the way whatever made it did.

You can take it from there yourself. You just don't get a chance to contemplate this kind of purity of spirit too often. Nobody *craves* the boogum, the elephant trees, the elegant cardon, or flowering century agaves. The land is useless for all but what it is. There is no other place like it in the world.

More and more, I've come to see that places like Baja have meaning beyond their surf and fish. Sometimes I can even get my mind around the notion that places *without* surf or fish can have meaning, too. I think this is a broader view. My wife, Kay, on the other hand, was never able to see it. She was always fearful in Baja, even in the middle of nowhere. She has heard the stories, too. Worse, she believes them.

The second thing everybody asks about is the fishing. Is it really as good as they say? I can honestly answer "No." Because the thing is, most guys you talk to haven't fished the surf with flies. They don't know how good *that* Baja story can be.

San Ignacio
From Sepic's Journals

*E*veryone who travels in Baja falls under the spell of San Ignacio. It is more than the shade, the palpable contrast between desert and oasis. Here, finally, it is possible to believe that humankind belongs on the peninsula, that its existence is maintained by something other than sheer willpower. In the severe mountains outside of town, aboriginal artwork clings to cliffs and cave walls. Along the plaza stands the purposeful eighteenth-century Dominican mission. Enormous ficus trees buckle flatwork beneath carts of vendors selling popsicles and sodas, the centuries-old roots tapping the same high water table that quenches the surrounding arroyo of elegant date palms. To stop in San Ignacio is to experience both a physical and an emotional response, a sigh of relief as one yields to the sudden anomaly of a place and time more closely akin to mainland Mexico, or a memory of Faulkner's make-believe South.

But there is another San Ignacio—or perhaps it is simply more of the same. Sixty miles beyond town, at the tail of this vast and barren Pacific watershed, lies the desert estuary of Laguna San Ignacio. Here, too, move reflections of the spirit of Baja, a wilderness dynamic that goes beyond the magnificent annual return of gray whales to their timeless birthing grounds. That's part of it, yes. Yet for those who have traveled in Baja at all, seeking something larger than themselves, San Ignacio lagoon offers a window beyond reason, history, and maybe time. Its rhythms suggest eternity, its stillness both magic and mystery. It's a long way from anywhere—certainly almost any place you've fallen for before. And it's an awfully good place to go fishing, stripping flies through the moving tides.

Four hours after leaving town—maybe more, maybe less—
even the restful shade of San Ignacio's anachronistic plaza
seems of another, more modern world. Now, skirting the edge of
the lagoon, you are *out there*. Depending on the season or the
year, you may be looking at a hundred square miles of bay and
wetlands, sometimes twice that, though much of the water
would be only inches deep. Across the flats to the north
stretches one of the driest deserts in all the world. Along the
foot of the mountains above the reaches of gumbo and quick-
sands, the road will have passed but a handful of sparse ranches,
each associated with a suspicious well or tenuous spring. Cattle
may or may not have been seen. Yet as you settle onto the level
of the lagoon, tracing that osmotic periphery between land and
sea, it is as though you have descended into a world unto itself,
a complete and whole ecology separate from any other. The
boundaries of that world seem more vertical than horizontal,
defined by the range of tides. Clearly, where you are now is
sometimes under water. You wouldn't be this close to the
lagoon, you wouldn't be so deep *in* the lagoon, if others hadn't
been there before.

Francisco Mayoral was one of many. Now he is practically the
last. In the old days, big fish camps crowded the edge of the
lagoon, rickety tents and *palapas* that would disappear in the
high waters of the random chubasco. But the lagoon was rich
with clams and cockles, crabs and shrimp, and even the great
sea-going turtles, the inshore baits and waves of pelagic fishes.
Livelihoods were made. Finally, however, too many became
dependent on the lagoon, and its circumscribed limits balanced
out at that level at which it could simply support itself. This is an
old story, one of the good ones without, so far, a tragic ending.
Because of the whales, the upper lagoon was closed to visitors
altogether, and the rest of it remains off-limits to commercial and

sport fishing—unless you first address Francisco Mayoral.

His house sits near the road, following a long, straight shot built up above a broad expanse of muck in which a vehicle could remain forever. Beyond Francisco's house, you can see the road gets trickier still. It is not only appropriate, but prudent that you stop. There is a flavor to these chance appointments, a sense of frontier communion that goes beyond negotiating permission or mere local formalities. My buddy Peter calls it "The Palaver." If nothing else, it's clear this may be the house you return to soon to ask for help.

We climb out of the trucks, my father and his pal Dave from a four-wheel-drive import, Peter and I from my thirty-year-old GMC, still tough enough in the ways that matter. Francisco comes outside and greets us, his house the only one visible for miles, the quintessential Baja house: square, squat, the cinder blocks unpainted, the dirt yard swept free of sand, surrounded by a low wall with geraniums potted in rusty coffee cans along the top. It's the sort of house you know has weathered it all. Francisco looks like that kind of man, too.

We present him with a gift, a nautical compass from a mutual friend in San Diego. Francisco shows less interest in three grocery sacks of secondhand clothing. When his wife comes out, it's apparent there will be no perfect fits passed along from the women in our own lives. She gathers the lot anyway with a smile and "Como no?" After helping with the clothes, Francisco returns, motioning with his head back toward the house and rolling his eyes. We ask if we can fish the lagoon.

I believe this one of the profound moments in sport. You've arrived at a man's home and expect him to share his game. Naturally, this delicate exchange can descend into shouts, finger pointing, or gunfire. It can also be an instant of sacred trust.

We gesture toward the little bay boat atop Dave's truck, then show Francisco some of the *plumas* cast with our fly rods. The equation does not suggest wholesale depletion. Francisco agrees, asking only that we help him fill out paperwork about our visit so that he can collect his salary in his role as nature-reserve watchdog, a small stipend paid by the Mexican government that helps defray the costs of his own fishing, the real source of food on his family's table. "Getting legal," it's called: the first step. It's a matter of following rules.

The road to the outer lagoon is worse than expected, deteriorating like bad fruit. If the tide weren't low, a minus, new-moon low, we wouldn't even be thinking about this. Still, we can gauge our course across the flats by sticks stuck upright in the mud, as far apart as telephone poles. When we get out and walk, the road actually feels solid, even if in places it lies a foot or two under water. Better yet, the road *surface*, if you will, is comprised of clam and cockle shells, the remains of that enormous pioneer harvest—an ingenious twist on recycling. Nevertheless, it's a full-tilt, say-your-prayers-and-hit-it run across the flats, windshield wipers wiping, and one truck finishes before the next one starts. Then the road fizzles out and disappears.

We get out and reconnoiter—"wreckin' goiters?" somebody says, giddy with adrenaline, to shared snorts and laughter. Anyway, we get out and look around. We're headed toward a secret spot, somewhere that a mutual friend from San Diego pinpointed on an ill-defined map in a ten-year-old *National Geographic*. It's safe to assume, now, that "secret spot" is a misnomer, an absurd concept in the face of more wilderness shoreline than any of us have ever seen from any vantage point before. Yet when a guy goes to all the trouble to tell me something like "Head straight for the graveyard, turn left at the pile of skulls, and look for the triangulation of seven dunes and the setting sun," I've learned to, you know, *listen*. Especially when that's all I've got to go on.

We head out across the pickleweed, advancing in that perilous balance between debilitating caution and fatalistic brinkmanship. We're going fishing, and we just want to get there—wherever *there* may be. Tracing a slender, tilted beach, we negotiate several hundred yards without further undermining our dental work. This is fun as long as it is happening to somebody else. Finally, we all agree on one last knuckle of land and set off along the water and just *go*. Bouncing over a shallow outcrop of slick mudstone, I suddenly recognize our source's description of his "fish camp." I ease off the gas just enough to glance around—and then my wheels are spinning.

I shut down. Dave crawls up behind me, all four wheels working. There's thirty feet between us and the high-water mark, and across the shallow inlet directly in front of us lies the mangrove. A low shelf of rocks stretches off into the lagoon proper, and in the other direction, the last little point I came waltzing over before—

"You stuck very bad?"

My father digs a toe into the sand and freshly-squished pickleweed, menacingly high on the pickup's old split rims. We go around and inspect the other side, a hot wind meeting us as we come out from behind the camper. The shell is already throwing off heat. Up in the *cholla* and pale dunes, you can see heat waves rising against blue horizons. Suddenly, it feels as if we are standing on an island, the shore of an actual island within the isolated ecology that is the lagoon itself. By the nature of the road just traveled, this sense of being totally surrounded by water may be more real than any of us cares to admit.

"Well, what do you think?" My father again nudges a tire with his toe. Another hot gust blasts us from behind. I can hear beer bottles opening. "Can you get out?"

"Well, we'll find out in a week, I guess."

This is a fishing story. By now it should be recognized, however, that here was the perfect antidote for the insatiable lusts generally associated with Baja trips. I've yet to describe a cast, strike, or "incredible surge of power." Like most anglers of recent generations, I've often succumbed to inscrutable whimpering based upon the singular belief that only in true wilderness can fishing be as good as it should be. It's mostly a feeling of having arrived too late. I'm writing this today in the Northwest, where my sense of tardiness may well be based on terrible truths. But in Baja, there remains that lasting impression of plenty—of bounty, abundance, and hope—if only in these places known by few but the patient traveler. For once, simply fishing the fly would be enough—regardless how many carcasses we hung, or "spent but dauntless denizens" we slid onto the beach. Which may sound like a long-winded way of saying we didn't make much happen. I guess it all depends what one really calls fishing.

There remains a feeling I want to capture about San Ignacio lagoon. There is the heat, and there is the wind, and there is that dizzying sense of promise that comes from setting off with a fly rod along wilderness inshore waters rushing with the pulse of tides. And then there is the mangrove.

For those who are intimate with the shores of Baja, especially the Pacific stretches and their inherent harsh and tameless ways, the lush greenery of the mangrove promotes visions of magical serenity set abruptly between barren sands and the painful deep blue of tidewaters. And to enter the mangrove, to dissect a small portion of it on the tongue of a flooding tide, is to come to know a flavor of the peninsula as exotic as its trout streams and mysterious lost missions. There can be no dissociation of locale greater than drifting in the fecund tropical stench of a Baja mangrove, the cries of yellow warblers piercing the rank air, pelicans and magnificent frigate birds coursing the impossibly blue sky. Imagine, say, banana trees in an alpine meadow.

Current swept the tip of the point beyond camp, rushing in out of the lagoon proper on the flood or pouring out of the mangrove and the little false bay as the tide receded. Which meant that there was a spot, rather precise, where a long cast could set a fly to work directly within the junction of these strong, intersecting currents. And at that spot, not surprisingly, there were usually fish of one sort or another—bass or halibut or jacks—so that all in all, this was just about as sweet a spot as any fly rodder could ever ask for.

But of course, we were really there to fish the mangrove. My father and I took the boat in on the second day. He and his pal Dave had poked around first, not finding much, while Peter and I partook in one of our typical long-range shore jaunts, not finding much, either. I was eager to crack the nut. So eager that I had us out in the boat at the first press of morning tide, which we rode as far as we could across the bay in the main channel. A hundred yards short of the mangrove, we ran out of water.

We staked the boat in the mud and I climbed out and walked the flats along the edge of the mangrove. My father, more patient with age, stayed seated, sipping coffee from the Aladdin thermos. I found a stick and marked the progress of the tide, as though the information mattered. A ways off toward the inlet to the bay, the mangrove was still draining, water flowing out the tail of a narrow creek and directly against the rise of the tide shrinking the exposed flats by the minute. The channel, widening, finally crested the flats ahead, water pouring into the mouth of the main tidal creek, so that where I was standing was within a complete loop of flowing water, at the very point of ingress and egress, the entire flush and drain and refill cycle of the mangrove ecosystem all taking place at once. Which is the kind of stuff you notice when you've nothing else to do but wait.

The boat floated and swung round on its rope. I climbed back in, briefly grounding us again. And for awhile, we sat there, looking, I suppose, like a pair of chess players in a bathtub. Let's just say we were ready to go fishing. The boat, a little aluminum

Klamath job never meant to "skim over dew," finally broke free for good, and we sort of poled and paddled into the tidal creek proper. Then my father yanked the outboard to life, and we got up on plane and swept round the first bend, crossing the threshold of the mangrove in the vein of the midmorning tide.

Little by little you begin to figure things out. Besides the fresh, untrampled marsh grass and pickleweed, our camp was set directly amidst an odd, stony refuse like nothing else encountered around the lagoon. Not only were the rocks unique, but they were all broken, split, such that many had sharp "working" edges. We were camped precisely where early inhabitants had come to collect and clean their harvest from these same waters. In the right light, it was easy to imagine work parties or seasonal camps spread out along the point, their movements reflecting an organic circulation throughout the immense, ancient midden piles. Casting from the tip of the point, the big fly swinging with current toward that exact sweet spot where each strike seemed to come, you were actually standing on a composite of sediment, silt, and shell, a sort of geological feature that may well have been man-made. In some respects, it was like fishing from the end of a jetty.

We also had to wonder if we were somehow disturbing this rich archaeological site. And there remained our cloudy arguments for fishing in what was really, after all, a nature preserve. Phrases like "delicate vulnerability" kept springing up in conversation. The mangrove proved the nursery for the lagoon's prevalent bass species. What we were hoping to find, of course, were snook, the *robalo* of mangrove legends. The second afternoon, we were visited by two of Francisco's buddies. I was just unsettled enough to imagine things might get sticky. They anchored their *panga* in the channel off the point, and then they set to cleaning a big haul of fresh fish, tossing heads into the bay. While working, they shared that there were no more *robalos* in the lagoon: the snook had all been caught by gill nets stretched across the mangrove creeks.

That evening, Peter waded with the flooding tide out onto the flats of our little bay, casting for fish of two and three pounds that we could spot drifting in the swirling eddies. For awhile, he was convinced they were some sort of surf fish, a corbina or corvina or the like, and he laid out long, gentle casts we could follow at the end of his floating line. This was picture-postcard stuff, the intense, low light showing every wrinkle on the water. We were all hoping just once he would lift tight to something solid. Yet we knew, deep down, that these were mullets—and that if we wanted any real shot at them, what was called for was a fly to mimic a frozen pea.

The wind blew these spells of fantasy into oblivion, at times cranking up enough to impress even the hardened Baja angler. Typically you can expect stiff afternoon onshore winds along the Pacific, and often even early-morning breezes blowing off the land, but the lagoon seemed subject to a more intense, short-fused machinery that settled down for but an hour or two before swinging right around and letting go from the opposite direction, without the usual warm-up period as things get realigned. Often, the offshore wind started before dark, whipping all through the night. Then, after a brief late-morning coffee break, the onshore flow just up and honked, shutting down sport like cops on a *calle de floras*. Which usually pleased us, considering what the heat was like when the wind ceased.

Surrounded by water in the harsh Baja light, our camp seemed heated as much by energy radiating off the lagoon as by direct rays from the sun. Something in that equation translates into the richness of the lagoon ecology, especially the enormous amounts of pure energy that must somehow be absorbed and transmitted into a nursery for whales. You don't think animals that size travel those thousands of miles each year simply because of, you know, *currents?* Then again, what but this kind of unfathomable wealth of energy are currents all about?

We managed the heat by nearly constant contact with water, and for the first time since snow skiing as a kid, I suffered a severe eye sunburn, my obstinance toward the use of sunglasses borne of a zealous pride in eyesight and twenty years of surfing without apparent optic harm—emphasis on *apparent.* The radiant light and utter lack of shade begged for an intense scrutiny of all liquid margins, which imprinted itself as retinal damage. I spent one afternoon in the wind devising an ingenious croakie out of Amnesia, the monofilament running line I use behind shooting heads, affixing it to an old pair of sunglasses with an elaborate combination nail knot and Albright Special. "If a job's worth doing," I proclaimed, "it's worth doing right!" Upon setting the whole affair in place, the knot immediately unraveled, inspiring the sort of dumfounded, blank stare on my part that can only be fully appreciated with the manic laughter that comes from far too many days in a shadeless, windswept Baja fish camp.

To be frank, we did go a little stir-crazy, a not atypical response to the severities of Baja and our grandiloquent efforts to do with fly rods what we generally assumed few if any anglers had ever done before. That's an awfully big bite to chew. One tide, I got into a pair of racehorses, or at least ponies, each going all bejesus out off the point, spurting into midair, to everyone's delight, though nobody's as much as my own. We called them *pamponito,* for lack of a better name. They appeared to be a type of jack, sleek and silver and pelagic. Later, Peter identified these fish as *Oligoplites,* more commonly known as leatherjackets, leathercoats, or leathernecks, the largest of which are said to reach fifteen inches. Well, I've got the photos to prove mine twice as long. But who really cares? Leather this or leather that, these little jacks could *go*. And after all is said and done, that's pretty much all you can ever ask of fish when you wade out and wave a long rod. That and maybe a good meal each day.

Okay, so I can't help it: I'm woefully addicted to telling tales of tight lines and "heart-stopping fish hammering flies while charging through the climbing tide." Next it'll be sex and gunfire. Whatever happened to the "ecological serenity of the mangrove"?

My father and I got into the baby bay bass, moving about in the mangrove as the spirit moved us. These were truly small fish—and after the novelty of the mangrove experience began to wear off, our more deeply rooted angling desires surfaced.

"Where the hell are the big ones?"

This would be about the same moment we heard splashing. We were anchored toward the middle of the tidal creek, in a big pool where a good cast could reach the edge of the vegetation along either side. The splashing, as far as we could tell, was up near the bend above us, perhaps within a little indentation under the overhanging mangrove. It was hard to pinpoint. We rowed over to take a closer look. Nothing was visible, yet now and then we heard another splash, and then another, each one like a heavy object—say a pipe wrench or a hardbound novel—dropped into a toilet.

But we couldn't see anything. Finally, my father had sense enough to pitch a fly that way. And not just any fly, mind you. This was some kind of Clouser Minnow, one of those outrageously heavy-headed flies that, if affixed to anything other than a fly line, would be appropriately called a jig. Such flies naturally cast about as easily as lead balloons, and they belong in that category of tackle peculiar to the breed of angler who will *stop at nothing*.

Maybe I'm just old-fashioned. Or in this case, jealous. What such flies lack in airborne elegance or lifelike drift is more than made up for by their ability to *get down*. This getting down is not to be confused with what people attempt to do on a dance floor, or what we wish the retriever would do when you arrive for dinner in your fine-twill suit. No, a fly that gets down is a fly that sinks, and sinks in a big hurry.

This was one of the few times I've ever felt a rocklike presentation completely outfished the more typical, animate fare. Or maybe it was just my father. It's not as if he hasn't done it before. He tossed the fly toward the sounds of splashing, and it plopped down among the tangle of roots and branches. I don't know if it was the first cast that broke things loose. But I do know it wasn't long before my father was into big fish, one after another.

One of the thrills of inshore saltwater fly fishing is the range of types and sizes of fish you encounter, all of which are at the very least amusing. It's a matter of intimacy. Up to this moment, there had been nothing lacking in our morning in the mangrove, just as one never feels actually shorted during, say, an evening catching native trout eight to ten inches long in an old-growth watershed. The point is, you wouldn't have been there fishing in the first place if it hadn't have been for that fly rod in your hand. And fly gear and small fish are a natural match, simply because of the proximity brought about by the reduction of scale. Yet in one instant, your perception of things can shatter—by the sight or feel of a fish that moments ago you would have never conceived as part of the close-up picture.

Among family and close friends, my father has long been referred to as Big Bob. Peter and I like to add "the Bass Buster" to that affectionate alias. This was a classic case in point. Where minutes before we had been diddling around with little bass scurrying about the pool at the end of our half-taut lines, suddenly, my father was called upon to put his weight into it, stopping something heavy dead in its tracks before it took him deeper into the mangrove, wrapped around the boat anchor, or exited via the other escape routes it attempted futilely to employ.

It seemed at first this must be a whole different species of fish, in the same way it's difficult to understand how, say, an Angel Cordero can be the same animal as Wilt Chamberlain. But these were replica bay bass all right, precisely the ones we'd been catching all morning, though upwards of ten times the size. I wondered what test tippet my father had on. It was all close-range infighting, no singing reel, about as subtle as cane poling. But you had to *stop* them. If my father hadn't, I wouldn't be writing this now.

He busted one big bass after another. I picked up one that was half the size of his best, then returned to catching infants. I'm never humiliated by such events, but you do begin to wonder. I guess I could have borrowed one of my father's Clousers— but the point of all this is never so simple a matter as doing just what it takes to catch the fish. And if any of us fall into the trap of believing there's only one way that works, we might just as well put away the rods and call up our accountants or clergymen and settle up matters here and now. Just don't ask me what the point actually *is*.

I knew we were going to get out. I knew we were going to get out and I knew we weren't going to have any trouble, because that's the kind of trip it was. Some are like that. Some aren't.

After a week back home, my father phoned one evening and said he'd been talking with a guy who couldn't understand why we'd traveled so far and so hard to nowhere just to catch some small fish we probably could have caught anywhere up and down the peninsula. It sounded like my father was asking me the question. I reminded him that they weren't *all* small fish—and that even if they had been, we caught them all on flies. And when's the last time he'd been fishing, I asked, in such unique, remote, *pristine* waters?

"I know, I know," said my father, sharing my impatience. "I'm just telling you what this guy said."

"Then it sounds like we don't need to worry about this guy going fishing there."

"No, we don't," said my father. "We don't need to worry about that at all."

There was a moment's silence, that crystalline nugget of understanding a father and son will share whether they like it or not. He *is* the Bass Buster. So what does that make me?

"Those were good bass you caught," I said, finally.

"That was a good trip," said my father. "I can't wait to go again."

Fathers and Sons
From Sepic's Journals

*T*here's a picture I keep in a stack of photos I pull out to impress new friends that shows my father on a beach in Baja holding a halibut he's having trouble lifting off the sand. Unlike me, my father is not a small man. In the hand not immersed in the gills of the big fish, my father also holds a fly rod. Though he didn't know it at the time, the rod was broken, the result of an awkward, impromptu landing. My father also looks pretty stoked. Although not one to peruse an IGFA record book, he *knew* the fish was special, more so because of how he had caught it. Only later would I inform him he could have shattered the existing world record four or five times over—even had he gutted the fish, loaded it into a gunnysack, and hauled it four hundred miles to the nearest official scale. *Folded* it would not have fit in a Coleman cooler.

This wasn't the first world-record fish I saw go unrecognized along the beaches of Baja. Casting flies into desert surf had opened a window into the extraordinary. Not that we were looking to make names for ourselves. The goal was sport and all its gnomic mystery. Fishing flies where flies might never have been fished before seemed merely the most sporting proposition going.

That big halibut took an oversized green and white Deceiver retrieved through sandy shallows beyond a tuft of rocks along a leeward beach we favored in the typical Baja afternoon wind. Camp stood in the scrub and stones above the high-water berm. Prophetically, my father announced on leaving that he intended to stroll down the beach and catch a halibut for dinner. I've been challenged on the notion of flounders as fly-rod sport. But the

California halibut was what got us into fishing artificials in the surf in the first place, their ambush feeding from inshore lies the perfect response to lures of any sort retrieved through their elevated strike zone. Out surfing, I've seen halibut explode through the surface, presumably ingesting their kill. And one need merely look at the mouth of the species to settle any doubts as to the validity of claims about their status as a predacious, fly-rod-worthy gamefish. The jaw itself seems able to unhinge, opening beyond credible limits in the manner of carnivorous snakes. Inside stands a set of needle-sharp teeth that are dangerous on even the smallest fish. The big ones are downright scary.

My father's bravado notwithstanding, he wasn't the most likely candidate for blowing a saltwater fly-rod record out of the books. Except for a time or two decades before, casting to bonito boils inside the Newport jetties, he'd had no experience with saltwater fly fishing until I began unraveling the code in the Baja surf. Even then, he was just as apt to pull out his beloved spinning gear, whether to toss chrome spoons along an empty beach or climb out onto headland rocks with a rubber-tailed jig to wrestle bass. I remember the first morning I guided my father into fly-rod surf fish, the cherry breaker a spirited yellowfin croaker at least double the local norm. Then he got himself an honest halibut, which took him into the rocks, up near a tide pool, and to the feet of where my buddy Peter and I stood watching. My father looked over at us as if expecting one of us to step down and grab the fish. But unless explicitly asked, we *never* touch another man's fish. My father then proceeded to stumble and fall. Peter and I kept quiet and our respectful distance. The seat of his pants now wet, my father gathered himself and finally slid the fish safely to where he could reach it.

"Watch out for those teeth," I said, just to make sure he did.

"I know," said my father. "I *know.*"

Still, to imply my father unworthy or even underqualified for that big halibut years later would be heresy. Because like most good anglers, he has always maintained the propensity to hook *and* land the exceptional fish—regardless of the tool in hand. And after the long fight, which eventually found him standing on a shelf of rock, staring down through deeper water at a tired, but dangerous wild animal, my father still faced the sort of moment for which nothing in an angler's past adequately prepares him.

There were no good options. My father suffered a moment's indecision. And as he leaned forward, rod in hand, inspecting the situation more closely, he watched the big fly detach from the halibut's mouth and drift slowly free.

It was enough to make the heart stop. Then my father hit the water. He took the only shot he had. Gills swallowed his fist, in a way no halibut's should, his groping fingers stopping just short of the big fish's toothy maw.

Now, as I said, when it comes to fly fishing in the surf, I've taught my father pretty much everything he knows. But let's get clear about it right now. I didn't teach him *that*.

My father and his father were Midwestern sportsmen. Which is to say, they loved to fish and to hunt birds. Remarkably, they moved to California with good split-cane fly rods, although my grandfather did leave behind his pointer and cherished .410. It wasn't long, however, before they discovered what Southland sport was really all about. Soon, they were spending evenings in my grandfather's garage, feeding sheets of three-quarter-inch marine plywood through the Craftsman table saw.

I didn't get in much on the fishing from the *Aksarben*, a precious, all-wood cruiser with a cabin to sleep four on the runs out to schools of yellowtail, albacore, and white seabass. By then, slip rates had skyrocketed beyond either man's monthly mortgage. And once a craft that size left the water, it was more work than sport to use for fishing.

So I went deep-sea fishing on cattle boats. Usually, they were half-day trips out of Newport or Balboa with my grandfather, who retired about the time I reached the age I could handle live bait, a stout rod, and a conventional-wind reel. Of course, I knew this was two-bit, minor-league stuff compared with *serious* fishing trips, when he and my father took off in the middle of the night, to return with a trunkload of albacore my mother would then spend days canning. And I never felt entirely comfortable amid the herds of gruff old men who seemed dissatisfied no matter how many fish they flung into their gunnysacks. On the other hand, I never went fishing anywhere or in any way with my grandfather when he didn't imbue our sport with a similar brand of utilitarian severity. If there were fish being caught, we were doing some of the catching, which was more than I could say about pier fishing.

Because I was young and raised not to disrupt adults, I was instructed in a simple, but effective style of bait fishing. I secured my anchovy and lowered it with a sinker directly to the ocean floor. Then I reeled up a few turns and waited. Rarely was I allowed to free-spool live bait on the surface, and I don't recall anybody on those boats casting jigs or feathers. My tactics meant I encountered bass or halibut or the like, which didn't turn me on in the manner, say, of a good bonito, which I still got hit by occasionally, proceeding to irritate everyone around me as I struggled to haul it to the gaff.

One time I beat these odds. On successive anchovies, I landed a pair of white seabass, the only ones caught that day. I was eight years old. The deckhand helped with the first as I was reeling away, taking up space and getting nowhere. He gave my rod back after determining it was adjoined to a fish, and not the bottom or a load of kelp. My grandfather simply kept directing me to keep my rod tip up, a command I heard throughout my childhood with the force and frequency with which I was also advised to keep my eye on the ball, whatever the ball may have been.

There was a period of anxiety during the run back to harbor. It was not uncommon for guys to bunk down below deck and then appear dockside with a bigger fish. Finally, I was handed the jackpot, twenty singles, including the first one ever entered for me by my grandfather. This was definitely *serious* sport, and I remember my grandfather carefully instructing me how to reveal the prize to my father.

It must have been a work day. A Southland sportfishing retiree wouldn't think to take his grandson cattle-boating on a weekend. And I know we went first past my grandfather's house, because I still have *that* photo of me on his back lawn with a death grip around a stiffened white seabass. Part of the deal was to make sure my father arrived home first. My grandfather wanted us to raise the trunk lid the exact same way he and my father would, after pulling in and waiting for someone to get around to asking, "Well, how did you do?"

You talk about your enduring images. My memories of those open trunks framing lumpy gunnysacks and pallid fish carcasses ignite the same internal commotion as recollections of early dating. I mean, those trunks were *cavernous*—not the sort of modern distillation that is all but useless for anything more than a wine magnum and a wheel of Brie. And sometimes our fish put an astonishing dent in those spaces, filling the dark reaches as if tortured souls on a Goya canvas.

As instructed, I waited until my father had turned up the prize seabass before unpocketing the twenty bills. He looked back and forth between the fish and the money, understanding sharpening his gaze. My grandfather just stood there, smug as a priest, the way he liked to when showing my mother a hundred pounds of albacore she now had to deal with.

When my father did finally did speak, there was that touch of perfect pride that no son ever heard enough of.

"How about that!" he said.

Now, would I contend there exists some genetic voodoo passed on to sons from fathers who fish—especially those who fish as if it matters? Only if pressed. Because my interest here is not so much in what is carried down from one generation to the next. Fishing, by nature, implies mysteries that radiate in all directions. Rather than what a son learns from his father, there soon exists something that resounds back and forth between the two generations—something that they share. So in time, the truly lucky fisherman learns about fishing from the son he taught, discovers, one day, he is student as much as teacher, finds himself, ultimately, with a new fishing buddy, such that the two of them have achieved a level of intimacy whereby they learn from each other, not as father and son, but as men.

My first son caught his first fish on a worm in Yellowstone. I love the blasphemy: *On a worm in Yellowstone!* But kids under twelve are allowed to fish worms in the upper Gardner drainage, a policy that both provides a benign introduction to the nation's sporting heritage, and, perhaps less altruistically, helps reduce populations of the non-native brook trout, that locally exotic char.

It was a strange trip, to start with. My mother and father had joined my wife and me, along with our four-year-old Speed, and, fatefully, a second child in the maternal oven. We were not the typical dawn-to-dusk, cast-'til-you-crash wader brigade. Also, upon arriving in the park, we discovered high water from nearly a month straight of June rains, plus closures on one of my favorite cutthroat streams due to grizzly activity, and, to my embarrassment, new regulations that I'd failed to decipher upon receiving my copy back home

In other words, I'd screwed up. And to be frank about it, my father and I spent days flailing about the park, suffering what can only be described as lousy fishing. Not that it was all bad timing. In the wake of continued exploits in the surf, everything about trout fishing seemed too small, too constricted, too *refined*. Which is to say, my trout game stunk. For days, the only fish I caught were small and stupid, most coming to the basic wet-fly swing, apparently all I could handle. I did raise one good fish one evening on the Gibbon in the Elk Park meadows, a solid fish that took precisely where it should as I was finally getting the hang again of presenting a properly floated dry. I fought the fish a long while, thrilled to have fooled and finally hooked the sort of fish we had traveled a thousand miles to encounter. Then it was gone.

The next morning on the Gardner, I rigged up Speed with a bobber on a length of leader tied directly to the top half of a fly rod. I dug worms for him from the moist bank above a likely looking pool. There's a lot of that water on that perfect little stream. By the time I got Speed's gear in order, a worm on his hook, and his bobber drifting smartly along an undercut bank, my father had lifted a pair of brookies from a bend downstream, the intensity of his casting increasing with each fish.

Speed's first was a replica of those same small trout. His bobber dived beneath the surface. I told him to keep his tip up. The fish darted about the pool, its excitement infecting ours. Then it was on the bank, flopping there in its nightmare of suffocation.

"Here, give me your rod!" I said.

I took the rod top and got the fish unhooked and down to the edge of the water. I told Speed to come look at it, exactly what he was already doing, squatting down beside me as I cradled the trout in the stream. It eased its way out of my hands, vanishing like a cartoon dream. Speed immediately stood up. He set off downstream. I called out and asked where he was going.

"To tell Opa I caught a fish!" he shouted, making for my father a half-mile away.

The following morning, our last in the park, my father and I made the long drive over to Slough Creek and finally stumbled into the Yellowstone magic. We'd been up in First Meadow the week before, fishing dark, heavy water under dark, icy skies. Now the season seemed at last to have changed, advancing a full notch, to where wildflowers and butterflies led us up the steep trail. We climbed into our waders at the edge of the trees above the meadow and set off through tall grass and a hidden marsh steaming in the morning sun. At a big oxbow, we each took a station at a ninety-degree bend, fifty yards between us. Soon I saw fish moving. Shortly after that, caddises appeared on the water, and I saw my father tight to a fish.

Three hours later, we both backed out of the stream. I pulled out a flask and handed it to my father. He asked me what it was, and I told him. We each took a drink. The hatch had pretty much ended, yet now and then another big cutthroat rolled, sending wrinkles through the riffle into the head of the pool.

"So now you know why we came here," I said.

"You've been saving that stuff to tell me *that*?"

Shadows creep at the margins of these lines. Finally, we may not be fishing so much as trying to insinuate ourselves into lasting impressions of love. Is it the backcast that actually determines the nature of the presentation? Or does the blessing of each angling generation reside in a quality of blindness that inspires faith beyond hope—or even prayer—each time the lure settles on the water? It really does seem enough to instruct our offspring how to fish. Yet none of us are immune to the temptation to dwell on the finality of the parted leader, the lost fish. Just as every father and son come to know, beyond all doubt, that there will never be an opportunity so simple as picking up to cast again.

We lost that second child my wife was carrying shortly after our return from Yellowstone. One day that summer, I dragged Speed along to a remote bass pond, a hike so long and difficult that by the time we reached the water, all he could do was lie down and sleep, then awaken and trudge back to the truck, one miserable step at a time. That same summer, on a road-day stop at Punta Chivato, I led my father on a twilight march beneath the rugged windward cliffs to a "secret spot" where I just knew I could scare up dinner. The thing was, I really wanted to fish alone. Within a half-dozen casts, I hung the meal, a big pargo wrestled out of the rocks with a Scampi and the jigging rod I called my meat stick. Such quick work, however, meant an immediate departure back to camp, yet another hour over loose shale and dislodged boulders, now hidden in darkness, a wicked track for any man, more so for one in his middle sixties who no longer sported a pair of healthy knees.

My father didn't walk the beach the next day. He stayed in camp, drinking coffee with his Advil and cursing me, I hoped mildly. I recalled yet another episode, from that period of unease that preceded my marriage, and, shortly thereafter, my grandfather's death. I'd been on the road, surfing and searching, a deplorable evasion of reality. Yet I had maintained enough sense to go fishing now and then. That fall, I put together a Sierra backpack trip with Peter, a late-season brook trout hunt to which we also invited my father.

We didn't do anything stupid. Because my father, even then, was slowing down, we kept to the east side of the divide, not attempting any of the rigorous passes without acclimation to either the heavy packs or the thin air. We also chose a drainage made up of a series of small lakes and tarns, so that if my father wanted to fish spinning gear, he could. He had begun to call me and Peter "purists." I didn't want that hanging over my head if he didn't catch fish. Soon, there was also friction over the matter of food: unpacking, we discovered nobody had the beef jerky, which meant my father's malamute must have grabbed it while we were at his house, divvying up loads. And then my father started complaining about raisins.

This is beautiful. My father, you see, had been at work while we did most of the packing, so when the three of us made the all-out search for the jerky, he was surprised to find those little boxes of raisins that kids and backpackers favor. And it turns out *he won't eat raisins*. Well, when it's your dog that's already depleted the group's caloric reserve by half, not to mention reduced the scope of cuisine to the option of scalloped card-board, you don't have a lot of room to whine about raisins. You may, in fact, consider yourself lucky you haven't brought that same dog along—even if you *are* fishing with "purists."

Then there were the blowed-up worms. This is terrific, too. Here we are, up in the pristine southern Sierra wilds, a little hun-gry and testy, it is true, but still, we're up there and fishing and getting small brook trout to rise to our flies, all in the spirit of sport, if not out-and-out love. Then, one morning, we spot a guy fishing along the lake below our camp, and we wander down to chitchat and see how he's doing. He's got his rod set in the fork of a willow branch stuck into the bank, and beside it is a lineup of dead fish to make your heart bleed.

Now I know these weren't wild trout. Most of them were "planted catchable rainbows," a category of dumb, vapid fish that has long supported the debased habits of a universal breed of angler. And what's the difference, really, between raising mam-mals for meat or fish for sport harvest and, presumably, consump-tion? Yet some of those trout were a decent, if not remarkable size, which meant they were probably holdovers from a previous season or two, and thus most capable fish, if not to spawn, at least to keep on living. Which is merely to ask, is it really in any angler's best interest to kill so many fish so quickly?

Still, my father expressed interest in these goings-on. He asked the fellow what he was using. The guy, about Peter's and my age, produced a Mason jar containing what looked to be a cross between canned green beans and pickled pig's feet.

"Blowed-up worms," he said, twirling the jar. "I inject air into them with a hypodermic needle. Keeps them floating off the bottom."

"Blowed-up worms," said my father, gazing at the dead fish. "I would have never thought of it."

Even if we'd had a hypodermic needle with us, I don't think

my father would have tried it. He really would stand on my side of the fence in these matters. Yet those little boxes of raisins he'd carried up into the mountains remained an issue. And he wasn't about to let two "purists" get off easy, not while he had chance to lord it over them by dint of a jar full of inflated, fool-proof nightcrawlers.

That evening, Peter killed two fish, spawning brookies dappled in strange, tropical hues. Each one had risen to an upstream nymph, fished in the film of a glass-clear feeder creek at the end of a fully greased line. We ate those two trout, lifting the shrimp-pink meat from the bones with the blades of our Swiss Army knives. My father, never one to relish fish, also seemed moved by the meal, unable to offer objection to the simple, perfect fare.

The last time my grandfather went fishing was with my father at Anaheim Lake, a suburban pond where senior citizens line up in lawn chairs and doze off in the Southland sun while waiting for planted trout to ingest their bait. Most of the men have their chairs outfitted with ingenious rod holders, which included battery-operated buzzers that go off in response to the tug of a hooked fish. This is about the minimum, sportwise. Yet it's generally agreed that this fishing is good for our old-timers, as if without it, they'd be roaming the streets smoking pot or chasing girls.

My father brought home fish that day in an ice chest and a Ziploc baggie. The biggest ones were notable by any trout standards. I remember inspecting those fish, and I remember thinking that this was great, my father still fishing with *his* father and the two of them still bringing home fish. Of course, there was no way I could have known this was the last such catch. And so maybe I can be excused for what came next—a brief, but pointed discussion of the relative merits of these fish and the two much smaller Sierra brook trout Peter had killed the previous fall.

"Which fish would you say were better?"

"What do you mean *better?*" replied my father, his tone inspired by my own.

"You know, *better.* Which ones were the better fish?"

No good can come of such talk. And I think we both should be commended for keeping the debate within the immediate context, refraining from any impulse to expand into morality, ethics, or religion. Because that's really what it was all about.

The shadows ebb and flow, flood and recede, the pattern of our imperfect faith. Deep in Baja lies a Pacific-side point with more potential for catching big fish out of the surf than any other spot I've heard of or seen. The first time I passed through, I was with Peter, looking for waves. We witnessed dolphins herding an acre of two-foot-long jacks into the cove inside the break, where they proceeded to feed like bonitos pounding a wad of anchovies. It took us several years to return, by which time the surfboards were playing backup to the fishing rods, some of which we'd built for casting the big flies that were allowing our wildest dreams to come true. Yet the very reason there are big fish skirting that point means at times a fly rod of any size is futile. The coast there bends abruptly, the land stretching far out to sea, so that the impression from the beach is more nautical than territorial. Stiff winds and open ocean swells course the point. The surf, at best, is always "just a little too rough." Long rods and big lures are often the call, and there is nothing delicate, effete, or refined about it. You wade out into waves, lifted off your feet during the sets. You wade a little deeper and let fly with your best shot.

The first evening that second trip, we cast spoons to big fish bodysurfing the shore break, the jack crevalle porpoising ahead until the whole wild scene would explode at our rod tips, washing us up against the steep beach and exposed, polished rocks. They might have been roosterfish. I caught a pair of the little jacks. The next morning we picked up porgy, basslike rock dwellers more brutish than sporting. Then Peter put it all together, going toe-to-toe with a big permit, the likes of which we'd never dreamed of, let alone seen.

Don't get me wrong: a fish like this would hardly get noticed on the bloodied decks of a long-range Baja cruise. We're talking here about *surf* fishing. A man wades into the sea and casts. It's as elemental as sex. And in the case of Peter's permit, caught out of wild waves and as brilliant as a full moon, it was a damn sight more heroic, too.

My father has never been enamored by my use of words like "heroic" to describe a certain type of fishing. Nor has my wife, who lumps any such angling reference in a category she calls "Romancing the Fly"—not a bad lick, if you carry the image right through. But this time, I've got to say the hell with them.

Our stay that trip was again all too brief, fit into a schedule between the long road south and hurried plane connections at the tip so that Peter and I could return to our families and jobs. But my father had a buddy of his own along, and after meeting up at the airport with their wives for a weekend of relative luxury, they returned to the point of Peter's heroics, bent on repeating the same. And my father nearly did. He hooked something heavy and was almost spooled, coming short of it only by cinching down the drag on a fish he claimed he never slowed.

"You mean you just couldn't stop it?" I asked later, sucking air at the thought of what might have been.

"No," said my father. "I never even slowed it down. That's what I mean."

"Maybe if you hadn't been using spinning gear? You know you can fight a fish better with a conventional reel. Even a fly reel. It's the simplest, most—"

"*I never even slowed it down*," repeated my father.

We went back one more time, just the two of us, me and my father, shortly after I'd agreed with my wife to move to Oregon to be near her family. We didn't make much happen the whole way south, and at the point, we ran smack into a late-summer chubasco parked two hundred miles offshore and pushing surf the size of nightmares from the horizon to the edge of our camp. We tried to wait it out. One afternoon, a surfer and his girlfriend came by and told us they had stayed there the week before, on their way down, and the water had been full of fish— so many that one morning he just paddled in, disturbed by all the big fish around.

"You *paddled in?*" I asked, incredulous on implications, as a surfer and angler both.

"He did," said the girl, glancing at the fellow with her own dismay, perhaps on grounds not dissimilar to my own. "He just all of a sudden paddled in."

"There were fish everywhere," injected the surfer. "And they were all *big*."

"And this was just last week?" asked my father, his heartache audible.

The surfer nodded.

"He paddled in," said the girl.

"He paddled in," I repeated to my father after the two had left—and again and again as the storm lingered on.

Finally we gave up and crossed over to the East Cape, setting up camp near a little headland where you could clamber out onto rocks at low tide and pick up fun fish on the fly. At least I could. For the first time, my father was unable to negotiate that sort of deal. The fly demanded difficult wading over unsure footing. And for once, his spinning gear let him down, his big lures obtrusive, too coarse for the game at hand. Tide after tide he tried. Cast after cast he got nothing. I was having the time of my life. My father kept talking about boats. The funny thing is, I listened.

First Season
Part Two
FROM SEPIC'S JOURNALS

*I*n traditional fly fishing," I intoned, "students were taught to cast holding a book between their elbow and side, a technique used to exaggerate the brevity of stroke required to deliver the fly properly. Done right, it's almost effortless. Or it should be."

I demonstrated the form, not my own, using a copy of *The New Yorker* with the article I'd been reading about Buster Keaton. I was inspired also to attempt my impression of the master's deadpan. Doctor Frank nodded, recognizing where I was going with this, although I'll hand it to him: he kept a straight face himself. My movements were accompanied by squeaking noises as the metal clasps of my new ectoskeleton pivoted against the tension of elasticized Velcro straps. I shortened my stroke further still. Relieved, I think, that this wasn't about work, pain prescriptions, or acceptable sex positions, Dr. Frank offered the opinion that it did appear that a man in my condition could cast a fly. But how did I intend to get to the water?

"Oh, you know, this is Oregon. There's water everywhere! Now could you go out to the waiting room and tell my wife what you just said to me?"

Kay wasn't as easy to convince. She had been in the hospital the day I first stood up. She claimed it took me twenty minutes to sit upright in bed, direct my feet to the floor, and rise. She also knew at that point, a week after the fall, that my plumbing remained out of order. Each evening, I was relieved by a catheter inserted by a nurse through sacred territory. Perhaps such details aren't vital to our story. On the other hand, I think they have a decided effect on a wife's assessment of a husband in my condition.

I was suddenly Kay's worst nightmare come true. At the age of six, she essentially lost her father when a logging-site cold deck collapsed above his head, not killing him, but crippling his mind. He never worked a real job again. That same year, Kay's two oldest brothers were drafted for the Vietnam War. Her grandmother died. Kay and two sisters and a younger brother were raised by her mother, her disabled father residing in the margins, the family cross, the smell of his pipe smoke stifling hope. This was a big reason Kay had left Oregon in the first place, taking flight to the Southland, come what may. Now the man she returned with was broken in the middle, the father of her two sons damaged goods, a companion supposed to share the load instead looming as the heaviest load himself. And what he seemed concerned about most was getting back on the water to fish.

I hesitate writing Kay's side of the story. Clearly, I'm not to be trusted. My perception is warped by a hapless need for approval. I want to be known as a guy with a good heart! Which means I'm subject to the lowest forms of deceit. A lot of what I write about fish descends into anthropomorphic nonsense, and what I have to say about others also can suffer the most fraudulent kind of projections. I can't even grasp the *concept* of truth.

Kay believes, at some level, I actually *intended* my fall. Two hours before it occurred, Kay informed Patch's nanny of the past year and a half since his abuse that she needed to make other plans. After months of deliberation, Kay had decided to stay home with the boys, open a day-care center, and trust the financial ramifications would work out. Then—*thud!*—the phone rang. As Kay stepped through the hospital-room curtains, the emergency nurse offered me an injection of morphine.

"He's not very happy," she explained. "This will help."

Dr. Frank and Kay and I stand conversing as a triangle in the spine clinic waiting room. Other patients appear more like high-tech industrial sculpture than respiring organisms on the mend.

Hell, I'm on my feet! I'm lucky, and I know it, and I return to my practiced song and dance about healing as a function of mind, body, and spirit: that the mere act of *going* fishing can inspire holistic benefits beyond any X-rayable alignment of bone or tissue; that an angler in surf or stream casting a fly into the very lifeblood that flows through nature is transposed by the vibrant forces that—

"Romancing the Fly," says Kay, nodding in my direction while looking at the doctor as would a mother appealing for patience for her disobedient child.

"He's pretty good at it," says Dr. Frank, offering Kay a hopeless smile.

"He's *very* good at it. What's frightening is, I think he believes it."

"Mmm," consoles the doctor.

Outside, Kay asks how dare I talk that way in public.

"I told you I didn't mind you going fishing," she adds, "as long as the doctors say it's okay."

"You argued when I said I could stand up and walk."

"You tried, but you couldn't!"

"I would have been able to if I hadn't have started to pass out."

"Your logic is impeccable," agrees my dear beloved.

"Keep your elbow still."

I wrap my arm around Speed, quieting his, my right hand reaching up to help with the rod. Snap it back, a foot, maybe less, holding his elbow tight to his side. It's the sort of discipline I can do without. On the other hand, sometimes we need to go too far, to the point of exaggeration, before returning with new understanding of what feels right, our own place of natural balance. I push the rod forward, trying to stop it precisely where it began. The line and short leader unfold in front of us, the fly tugging an instant before settling onto the stream.

"That's a real cast," letting go of the rod. "Now you're fishing."

The little dry drifts freely through the soft water inside the bend of the pool. I straighten up, my new denier waders shifting loudly over the straps of my brace. It's late September, three months after my fall, and the North Fork flows low and clear, deliciously gentle in all but the tightest, steepest runs. It may be the last trip of the season, and Speed and I have hiked up this morning from the high bridge, bushwhacking into headwaters and ribbons of stream, the heavy deadfall, toppled giants, and ancient debris directing current every which way, the shallow pools and deep, deep shade teeming with baby trout.

Speed turns back toward me, asking if he should cast again. The little fly leaps off the stream and jets overhead. Speed waits, patient as a man with a stop watch, then shoves the big rod forward, his elbow following, but mindfully far behind.

"Like that?"

"Just look at it," I say, pointing at the dancing fly. "You're fishing again."

The small cutthroat circles back and thrusts and smacks the fly. Speed manages the rod to vertical, pale legs coming out of the clear stream. He steps back over the cobbles, his tattered aquasocks helping, and drags the fish across the surface, guiding it my way.

"Perfect! Absolutely perfect!"

I squat down against the strain of waders and brace and bad back, getting the fish free and immediately back into the stream. I hold the rod a short ways up and work it to dry the fly.

"You're back in business," again letting the rod swing free.

"Pop?"

Speed stops the rod. The fly and leader fall at his feet.

"I'm cold, Pop. I'm really cold."

I help Speed dry off, rubbing his sweatshirt over his bony, eight-year-old legs, blotchy like the limbs of a surfer climbing out of a wet suit. We stand there in the warm sun, tiny trout dimpling the surface of the stream. Speed adds he's hungry, tired, and still really cold. I get it.

I guess you could say that trip was a big deal. Maybe I've reached the age at which they all are. For the first time, Speed fished the fly, practically on his own, and Peter had flown up from San Diego to join us, our first chance to explore what it was going to be like now that we were fishing buddies living a thousand miles apart. At the airport, I was startled by Peter's appearance: a goatee and scurvious short hair that hinted at self-infliction. Or thoughts of serial murder. I wasn't exactly a mirror image of the Dalai Lama, either, what with what I felt I'd been through since the move north, my own brand of bristlecone crewcut, and the special aspects of tensile-strength plastic exposed through the front of my Smith & Hawken garden smock, a bad Christmas gift that finally found its way out of the back of the closet because it was all I had that fit comfortably over my brace.

"Hank Stamper?" inquired Peter.

Speed and I meet Peter and his brother back at camp. John had arrived the previous day, pulling in just before sunset, eighteen hours behind schedule, and I had turned the two of them loose on the best water, giving them the chance to catch up on their own where it doesn't even matter if you raise a good fish. Now we build sandwiches out of hard salami and Tillamook cheddar and Walla Walla onions. While Peter eats, he sets up two vises, side by side, at my rickety camp table. I quickly pull out my own, feeling like a man on vacation for having just the one.

"Big dries," announces Peter, squeezing tight a second size 10. He starts his thread onto both hooks, leaves the pair of bobbins hanging, twirling slowly in the same direction. "All the big small ones I got hit big dries."

Peter leans back on his stool, studying the two empty hooks while hand rolling a cigarette. He's not a smoker, but you know how it is when guys go fishing. The impulse sharpens around a camp vise. We've got to get down to *creating*.

The big Diamond Blue Tip strikes the table. There's that first recognition of why the nasty habit was rejected, followed by second, more tolerant thoughts. Peter sits forward and picks through a Tupperware bread container, coming up with a pair of necks and swatches of fur. He ties both flies simultaneously, shifting back and forth between steps in rapid succession. I'm again intimidated by his speed. While I'm still aligning a hook in my vise, Peter spins his two dubbing loops and winds both bodies, tools whirling as a blur. Each pair of wings stands up straight the first try; the hackle spreads out as if light from a star. Executing his whips, Peter's hands look like a boxer's on the speed bag.

"Think I'll, uh, try some sort of caddis," hoping to catch up a little by not having to tie in a tail.

Peter snaps open each vise, catching the big flies as they fall. Then Lucy strolls up, pokes her nose onto the table, and snatches one of the necks, a sixty-dollar Grade No. 1 Metz variant.

"Hey! Grab that—"

I remind my best friend of the presence of a child.

"He can help."

We do the Chinese fire drill, finally corralling Lucy in the tent, where she suddenly becomes more interested in the pair of long johns Peter has been wearing the past three days under his waders. How can you possibly blame them for such refined instincts, born of nearly two hundred years of breeding?

"She's an idiot," argues Peter.

"She's mine," I confide.

I finish my fly, a honker on the order of a piss-stained bottle brush. Then Speed asks if he can try tying one himself.

I'm stoked, tickled he wants to, isn't really cold anymore. I get him set up with a hook and a bobbin, help him to start the thread. This isn't the first time for Speed: already, he's inspecting materials, toying with rhymes all his own.

Yet I can feel Peter peering over both our shoulders. Oblique smoke rings drift through my peripheral vision. No doubt he should be the one doing any teaching. My part in this sort of educational venue has always been at best that of the motivator, the encourager, the inspirator: "Stay low and shoot from the hip!" In contrast, Peter assumes there's value in real information. A hands-on scientist by trade, he finds it appropriate to communicate the details of craft and execution. Still, this is my son, and I figure it's not all about how well we are taught, but also by whom.

Speed, bless him, accepts the moment for what it is. He spins his old Padres cap backward and bears down on the fly with fated intensity, his pale eyes fixed on his work. Little does he know of my illusory handicaps. I look down at his stout thumbs, a family trademark, thinking of tools for which they seem particularly well turned: the hammer, tin snips, a brick trowel, or, yes, even a fly rod. But at the vise, they appear more of a liability, on the order of employing a pickup truck on your first date. Nevertheless, the fly takes ready form, a generic soft-hackle wet, straightforward as a button, a series of clean half-hitches at the head.

"Can I name it?" Speed dabs precisely with the bodkin.

"Go ahead," I sigh. "No one else has."

"How about 'The Edge?'" Speed's eyes fill with an easy self-delight, a painfully accurate reflection I recognize all too well.

Peter and I exchange looks.

"He's his father's son," Peter notes, opening the ice chest. "They don't fall far from the tree."

Despite pride and the beer I conclude out loud that nobody would get it.

"But if you can tie them fast and cheap enough—"

"Like Woolly Buggers!"

I hold Peter's gaze another moment. "What about a soda for the artist?" Which naturally leads to a toast all around.

"Sepic's Edge!"

Whereupon Speed says, "Pop?"

"What's that?"

"I don't understand what you two are talking about."

Peter raises his eyebrows.

"You're a sharp one, Speed. Ever since that root canal, I can't understand a word your dad says, either. I wish he'd been as lucky with his dog as he was with you."

Speed's eyes settle back onto the fly.

"Do you think it'll catch a fish?"

Given the choice, who would I rather fish with: friend or family? Or myself? This is not a rhetorical question. I believe I need to pay attention to what I'm doing and why. I don't recall receiving any sound instructions in how to make my own life work. Sometimes, the fly rod feels like a shoehorn, and I'm trying to squeeze myself into a size 6 AAA. I mean, I know fishing used to fit easily into my life, but I refuse to accept that means I was smaller. I hate that kind of judgment, placing fatherhood above friendship, age over youth, the decent livelihood above risk for, well, risk's sake. I know I suffer anger, defensiveness, depression. But maturity isn't the solution if all it demands is I *submit*.

My father has often observed that Peter and I have "a way of talking" from which he feels excluded. I'm trying to teach my children—as well as learn myself—that we are never separate from anyone else unless we choose to be. This is the sort of metaphysical quicksand into which fly fishers often sink. But if I don't love who I'm fishing with, how can I love myself?

We spread out that evening from camp, Speed herding Lucy along the margins of the stream, trying to stay dry before nightfall. I settled on a pair of linked pools, the top one more of a broad, even stretch of dry-fly water, the lower a classic spillway at the head, followed by a long, deep bend against a steep, brush-lined bank. For some reason, I had never fished this second pool in a way that felt right, always coming at it from the top or at the end of a session, when I wasn't really keen, thinking just as much about camp nearby and a cold one for my efforts. And after taking the one good-sized fish that spring—my only remarkable fish to date that first season on the North Fork—I had been swinging big, heavy nymphs through just this sort of pool, getting fun fish, it is true, but not another I could honestly call a thrill.

So of course this one was. I walked the length of the pool and squatted down on the cobblestones alongside the tailout, trying any new position to relieve my back, aching after another full day without removing my waders. Then, in a stroke of inspiration, divine guidance, or dumb luck, depending on your point of view, I tied on an outrageous fly for the occasion, a version of Bill McMillan's Steelhead Caddis, half again as big as anything we had tied that afternoon. I stood up and made a few casts, reaching into the top half of the pool. Then I moved up a half dozen paces, shot for the sweet spot at the very edge of the spill, and the moment the big fly lighted, its muted sunrise body gleaming through strands of pale deer hair, the big fish flashed through the surface like a flame through film.

"Oh my," I announced, without wondering to whom.

John said later he could see the fish jumping, watching it rise into view from where he was casting two pools upstream. He also said it was my hollering that caught his attention in the first place. So I don't know if I can believe him. I do make noise while into a good fish, but I want to think it's more on the order of the tree that nobody hears fall in the forest. Or is it the sound of one hand clapping?

And then there are the questions about the fish. Does it hear my excited voice? Do my silent shouts communicate feeling? Have I become suddenly *real* to the fish? Or does the fish fucking care what's going on, other than trying to escape the sharp, cold steel in its mouth, drawing it interminably away from its home?

This one was a matched bookend for the one at the start of the season. It never crossed my mind to kill it. I feel dangerously close to joining the words "symmetry" and "sublime": big wet, big dry; bottom, top; spring, fall; beginning, end; death, life. There you have it. I rocked the fish gently back and forth in the current, cradling it until it moved off on its own power. Then the trout vanished, eclipsed by the lens of the North Fork at dusk.

"Very poetic," offered Peter. We were the last two around the campfire, sipping wine from enameled metal cups. He has heard my accounts before. Lucy's at his feet, and now and then I notice his fingers reach out and scratch behind her ears.

"Now tell me. Are we going to find some real fish on the Deschutes?"

We did, but we didn't catch them. Smaller fish, though real enough in their own right, made nowhere near the impression of powerful apparitions disturbing the gauzy sageland twilights. One fish did show enough contempt for our offerings to carry Peter out around a snag and leave him there, shaking. I take this way too personally. So did Peter when Lucy, set free from her leash, entered the realm of shadowy trout feeding heavily in the dark eddy at his rod tip, opening the surface of the river as if artillery fire were tracing the margins of his casts.

Something was going on here. Isn't it always? The next day, John and I each managed an occasional foot-long redside, disappointing in the midst of so many big trout, although I will say John did make the most of his, spending the kind of time with each that indicates a man who is in no hurry to rush even the little things in life. Or who expects to live to be three hundred. Even Speed hooked up, twice losing small jumpers that slipped free of the classic Kamlooper spoon he had picked out for his spinning gear from John's early-career collection of Hot Shots, Dardevles, and the like.

But for Peter, there was nothing except the one abusive hookup, followed by the malevolent performance of my dear, purebred dog. You can go to the wall thinking about such things—though naturally, we all like to report that "going fishing is what it's really all about it. Catching fish just *enhances* the experience." This reasoning tastes worse by the hour if you happen to be the one guy getting skunked. And, anyway, I've come to feel a certain, well, *compassion* for the people I fish with—be they family, friend, or the fellow next door.

So I'll confess I prayed for Peter that last evening on the Deschutes, twelve hours before we parted again for I didn't know how long this time. If you're troubled by the notion of prayer, picture the big water and sky, the high, sculptured canyon walls, falling light, dark, heavy rainbows beginning to feed. Now add three men, all fathers, a son, a dog, and the rods. The spirit in all of this pretty much covers my faith. I kept Lucy on a short leash while I fished, finally dragging her out of the river after landing a last little trout. Peter cast beyond the edge of night, tying on one final fly while holding a flashlight in his teeth. And he raised a fish! I saw him strike, snap the rod up, his silhouette sharp against the traces of light remaining above the canyon wall. Then, slowly, painfully he reeled in slack line. He held his rod up and tried to make out the leader. I watched his hand reach, grab hold, follow the taper down to where the fly should have been. I saw the anger go through him, like waves of high voltage through a man already dead. The only question was whether or not my prayers had come from an honest heart, that place where compassion isn't just another form of our congenital self-delight. That, at least, had been answered.

Cane
FROM SEPIC'S JOURNALS

*F*or as long as I remember, there've been four cane rods floating around my family. One belonged to my father, and still does. The others were originally owned, respectively, by my dad's brother, their father, and *his* brother, Uncle Wen. I think I've got that right. Today, those three rods belong to me, or at least they did until I recently stripped and rebuilt one and gave it to my buddy Peter. Of the other two, one always goes along with me when I'm headed for trout water, although I can't recall, precisely, the last time I actually fished it.

The final rod of this quartet is, quite frankly, beat to shit—perhaps beyond repair. I'm going to get to that. But it isn't the point here. What I'm interested in is the spirit of some fine old fishing rods, a thread of hope that transcends any notions of loss. I don't care to dwell on tragedy, and sad songs aren't selling this year. There's enough bad news already.

My father likes to tell the story about the time years ago in Michigan a guy in a fly shop offered him a hundred and fifty bucks to hang his rod on the wall. The deal was, my dad could still come by and use it anytime he wanted. The guy just figured it was worth the money—in those days a bundle—to have a classy rod like that where all could see. I get it, but then I don't. I mean, did the guy think he would do more business because customers would be *jazzed*? Or did the rod turn *him* on? Or was it, simply, an attempt at a certain look, the likes of which are now essential to fashionable fly shops everywhere, providing the best excuse for requesting—if only metaphorically—that paying customers reach for their wallets.

I can get caught up in image, too. I remember the first time in Yellowstone, when Peter and I still carried our flies and what-not in old canvas Arctic creels, walking through Slough Creek Campground thinking, "Whooa . . . I guess I gotta get myself a *vest.*" And the first time I ever hired a guide, an experience not unlike the loss of virginity, I quieted my fears by reassuring myself over and over that regardless of all else, I would be looked upon with a modicum of respect, due to the fact that I was casting with a fifty-year-old split-cane classic, outfitted no less with a new cocobolo Struble reel seat. Either that, or I'd be just another Valley Cowboy, or some such schmuck.

I was in New Zealand on the way to a sister's wedding in Australia. (It's not as if I get to go to these places just to fish.) My wife had friends from college living in Auckland, and they found me the name of a guide up in Turangi. They also loaned us a car. New Zealanders love to show off their great country. We had Speed along, and we found a little room-and-kitchenette combo within sound of the Tongario River. It was April, *their* fall, and the big rainbow spawning runs out of Lake Taupo were gearing up.

I fished an evening and a day on my own, convincing myself, as is often the case, that I didn't know my backside from a hot rock. Then I called Frank Harwood. On hearing where I was from, he suggested we do some "small-stream" fishing. I said that sounded fine by me. He said if money was an issue, we could still probably count on getting into fish on a half-day hire. I said that sounded fine by me, too. Then Frank Harwood said we'd be sight fishing for rainbows running three to five pounds, and how did *that* sound? "Fine, Frank, fine," I said, suddenly finding it difficult to breathe freely. "That sounds fine by me."

It was more than just the money—though I must admit it did seem extravagant, spending as much for a morning's fishing as it would cost for a week in Baja. Kay agreed it wasn't cheap. But what took my breath away was the sudden image of casting on command for big, small-stream rainbows under the all-knowing gaze of a severe, clipped-accented, dry-witted colonialist sportsman, complete with pipe and probably the chiseled good looks and extraordinary skills and ethics of a Roderick Haig-Brown.

Well, Frank Hardwood doesn't smoke a pipe. This omission was more than made up for by the fine retriever he brought along, which he controlled along the stream by almost imperceptible gestures of a hand carried at his back. His other hand was often on his hip, clenched into a fist as he watched me cast, time and again, my lovely vintage fly rod, blowing off fish after fish until I could just *feel* Mister Harwood's pipeless jaws ache.

The scenario, oft repeated, went something like this. Walking upstream—a jewel of a creek, twisting low and clear through woods of ferns and broadleaf evergreens, as moist and achingly sweet as scenes in southern coastal Oregon—Frank would spot a fish, which I was able to locate only later, peering over Frank's shoulder and sighting down the length of his arm. Then I was told to approach carefully and cast. *False* casting was strictly taboo. The fish were all in the shallows, spooky as wrens in a marsh. It was the quintessential fine-and-far-off gig, made more difficult by the fact I was fishing *two* weighted nymphs, basic copper-and-peacocks at both the point and the dropper. I'm not going to go into the kind of remarkable knots I spun into this unwieldy terminal arrangement, other than to say that a time or two even Frank was impressed. Mostly, though, he simply stood to one side, watching until my misguided line or plopping nymphs drove the fish entirely off of its lie.

At which point Frank would raise a hand and step forward, announcing the disappearance of another trout, so we might as well move on, his other hand motioning directions to his dog with perturbed, cryptic precision.

I blamed my rod for my problems: the weighted nymphs felt as if I were trying to control a pair of bricks with a pencil and a kite string. Frank agreed, stating that, yes, with these old rods one does have to be *positive*. He took the rod and showed me what "positive" means. I noticed, among other things, how he choked up when casting a short line, relying on crisp, abrupt strokes to load the rod while keeping those heavy nymphs moving in one direction and in line. I know this sounds all too basic. But sometimes you do feel like you're starting out all over again. Frank moved up toward a pretty little slot, one of those classic kinks in a stream that just begs for a shot, even if you don't see a fish, slid his hand down onto the meat of the grip, stripped off line, and picked up and cast, not really reaching, but definitely airing things out some. The whole affair unfolded like verse, the two nymphs entering the water like a pair of linked BBs. The effect was positively beautiful, indeed.

I still don't know if he took me to that spot just to show off that cast.

"Nice stick," said Frank, smiling over a shoulder at me.

Of course, I did finally get into fish—I'm rarely bold enough to write about it when I don't—rainbows like chunks of two-by-four coursing the dimensions of the small stream. Even then, Frank objected to how I held my rod while fighting fish. The guy was an absolute *taskmaster*. Suffering one of the most stressful days of my angling career, I stated emphatically that what I really wanted to do was fish with Frank the next morning, too.

He called that night and said he'd just had a cancellation. Did I still want to go? Again we carried the one rod between us, but this time Frank Harwood fished *with* me, the two of us taking turns. Toward the end of the second morning, Frank even kept a fish, a bookend match with the one I planned to take to my wife's friends in Auckland. I hadn't killed a trout in years. Frank said you could still do that kind of thing there.

That afternoon, I shook hands with Frank outside our little room in Turangi. I said we'd have to do it again some year, which is probably what Frank always hears the last time he sees most visiting fishermen. Then he handed me my rod.

"Bring that stick back with you," he said, raising his hand as if playing a fish. "But get yourself a good graphite, too. We don't want to spend *all* of our time untangling flies."

Frank Harwood waved, his other hand motioning his dog back into the car.

It's impossible to state unequivocally what the allure of cane rods really is. Granted, they're cool as all get out, and to a point, I don't see a thing wrong with feeling groovy—if you'll excuse my French—while out for sport. Those in the know love the way cane rods cast, often getting teary-eyed and blurry of speech when relating the exquisite *ease* with which such rods deliver the fly, generally in a situation in which the narrator hooked a big, difficult fish shortly thereafter. And John Gierach writes some funny stuff about owning and using bamboo rods. But then, John Gierach writes funny stuff about a lot of things, which is why we read him, not because he and his friends like bamboo rods, or because they catch a lot of good trout with them.

Still, for my money, the quality that lifts a cane rod head and shoulders above the rest is its ability to hook, play, and land fish successfully. If I wasn't so fearful of rejection, I'd call the bamboo rods I own my very best trout-killing tools—although by "killing" I simply mean getting the job done. Which in my book is what cane rods do best.

I just don't recall breaking off many big fish with cane. Of course, I can forget my wife's birthday, too. But cane rods are as gentle as prayer on tippets, especially those treacherous wisps we generally have to resort to these days to fool fish. Yet that very same rod has no end to its backbone, offering greater and greater resistance the deeper the bend goes. How these two seemingly disparate attributes mesh as one is what in some circles is known as art. Or, if you're not careful and fish cane too much, the harmony can elicit notions of the divine. Often you can finish even that nasty fish double your tippet strength simply by snugging up on it and letting it beat itself up on the rod.

I know that doesn't sound pretty. But I don't think it hurts to remind ourselves now and then—even in these enlightened times of widespread catch-and-release attitudes—what it is we're really doing out there. And the fact is, quieting a fish into submission by *discouraging* it is probably more humane than having it exhaust itself to the point of toxic suffocation, and a damn sight healthier, too. Plus, I don't care what anybody says, leaving the fly stuck in the fish's mouth is just short of assault with criminal intent. We all do it. But I don't think we should ever feel *okay* about it.

Once, at Silver Creek, Peter and his brother and I got into one of those outrageous midmorning hatches that brings every big fish in the stream to the surface, but not a one would rise within a foot of my flies. We were more than a week into a whirlwind trip, and I was down to the low end in my precious supply of tiny dries, always the first to go. I should have just run back to the van and twisted up three nice ones. Anyway, I finally reached my frustration point and wandered downstream to where Peter's brother John had positioned himself such that he was getting a good drift through a tight bend and slot and all sorts of other promising wrinkles. Peter showed up and joined me. The next thing we know, John is into a heavy fish, and we're just dying, hoping he pulls it off and nothing goes haywire.

Now, John's a really careful guy. Peter calls him *slow*, which is also true, because the way John sees it, if you don't move too fast, you aren't apt to make many mistakes. Of course, it's hard to imagine what could go wrong when you're putting on your waders—yet more times than not, either Peter or I have to tell John to get it in gear, we're going fishing. And I know I've never seen anybody take longer landing a twelve-inch fish than I did watching John this year on the Deschutes. But as I said, he's really, really careful.

Which is why I was so surprised that morning on Silver Creek when John, a long time into that fish, broke it off. Say what you will, I fully believe that nine out of ten hookups that result in a parted leader are our own fault. Perhaps there's an old, worn religion raising its condemning head in that belief, but I just can't forgo my responsibility in the matter when a fish breaks off. I know all about big, badass steelhead or wild and gnarly jacks, but if that's the kind of fishing you're used to and you're still breaking off more than the random bad-luck one in ten, then you *really* need to take a close, hard look at where you are with your game.

Well, when John broke that fish off, Peter and I collapsed to our knees and covered our faces. It was that painful. John, bless him, just shrugged his shoulders, looked over, smiled, and waded out of the stream. Peter changed places with his brother, setting up precisely where John had been able to produce that good, effective drift.

I'm not sure what followed. All I know for certain is that Peter stood in that one spot and hooked and broke off three big fish in row. It was brutal. Then I remember it occurring to me that Peter was fishing a new graphite rod, and that he'd broken off more than his share of fish that trip. Something was amiss. Granted, these were heavy, hard-hitting rainbows, and I'm not going to sit here and argue that Peter would have landed any or all of them with a cane rod or even one of his old, pliant fiber-glass jobs. But, I mean, come on—and I can say this because Peter is my dearest friend—*three in a row*?

When I broke my back and suddenly found myself with a lit-tle extra time on my hands, I pulled out the cane rods for inspec-tion to see what I might be able to do to get them all back on the water. The one I learned to fly fish with, a production South Bend that may now be closer to sixty years old than fifty, was in with my current gear. That's the one that goes with me: it's caught trout in every state that I have, as well as in Mexico, and of course in that dreamy little stream in New Zealand. Still, this time I took a moment to draw it out of its tube and poplin rod bag, just, you know, to *see* it—and to make certain both tip sections were intact, not missing any guides or a top or something else I might have failed to take care of the last time I had it on the water.

Then I steadied myself for a close, hard look at the other two. How they came to be in my possession is beyond me. I believe my father would contend it was part of some sort of private conspiracy. But that isn't the case at all. Grandpa's been dead nearly a decade now, Uncle Wen died at least a dozen years before that, and *my* Uncle Dick lost interest in such things even before then. I have this general feeling of these family fly rods just falling into my lap—though of course, things don't happen like that. Or maybe they do.

What became clear as I looked over these other two rods, however, was that their care had been a responsibility at which, up to this point, I'd failed miserably. I'm not sure I deserve all the blame. I really don't remember destroying but the one. Yet in combination, I was looking at no less than a half-dozen sticks of split-cane rod in various states of disrepair, from pieces missing a ferrule or tip top to a couple that looked as if they had been fed into an industrial-strength garbage disposal—a collection of tweaked, maimed, and even splintered rod parts, their numbers exaggerated by the fact that these were three-piece rods, each with two tip sections, besides.

I tried swapping pieces around, hoping to come up with a combination out of which I could get one serviceable rod. No wonder I hadn't done this before. Finally, I gave up and said the hell with it. I drove to the nearest fly shop, one of *those* shops where you can spend a hundred bucks just thinking about what you might need, walked straight to the counter, and started talking.

"Hey, look, I gotta couple old rods here I'd like to see if I could maybe...."

Okay: it's probably too late here to put much giddy-up into

the story about how I more or less destroyed one of four heir-loom fly rods my family and I were blessed to fish with all these years. And I really don't know if it was ever much of a story at all. As I said, there's enough bad news already.

My wife and I were up in the San Pedro Martir mountains of central Baja, that surreal setting of granite and pines and alpine meadows. We were looking for trout, Baja's native *Salmo nelsoni*, which explains why I had a fly rod with me in the first place. Why that wasn't the same rod I'd been fly fishing with since day one, I don't know. Why, in fact, the rod I carried that trip just happened to be one of the *other two* cane rods that so serendipitously fell into my possession is also beyond my expla-nation, and may or may not have any import at all in this story, or even in what eventually happened. But it probably does.

The heart of the matter is this: my wife and I didn't find any trout, trout water, or anything resembling the two. Twice we even had difficulty finding water to drink. We also never really knew where we were, having set off with packs after leaving the Ford along a meadow that wasn't the same one we assumed we were starting out from on our map. Along the way, while leading my then wife-to-be on a wild-goose chase that more than remotely threatened our lives, I also had the unique oppor-tunity to watch myself demolish a precious fly rod as good as any I'll ever own.

I remember thinking after I broke the rod the first time that it would still be okay, the trout we were looking for weren't sup-posed to be very big, so I could probably make something work, even if it wasn't, you know, *perfect*. That's pretty much how my mind was functioning the whole trip. We made love the first afternoon out, spreading our bags on a little grassy nub above a trickle of a creek, and for awhile, Kay was self-conscious about someone happening by and seeing us. This, mind you, in the obscure reaches of some of the truest wilderness I've ever entered, where trails, if they exist at all, are made by game and, perhaps, the occasional vaquero.

"There's nothing," I said, "to worry about." Then I broke the rod some more.

Coming into the trip, I had figured it was going to be a stroll in the park, like climbing into the High Sierra: you know, you don't want to carry too much, you lash your rod to the side of your pack, you hike a few hours, and then you're up there and you're fishing and what could be easier than that? Well, we had to burrow through tangles of scrub oak and manzanita, plus negotiate the declivitous curves of countless granite boulders. And then, when you keep discovering that things don't line up as you thought they would, when the stream you figured would be flowing left is flowing right, when up becomes down, and the map you are holding makes as much sense looked at from any direction, well, you begin to make bold assumptions, extrapolations upon extrapolations, and these, naturally, mean that where you want to be is *over there*, not right here, so that means you have to climb over *that*, and the only way to do that is to go up *there*.

The rod kept breaking. Finally, I laid the pieces on the map with the compass and I took a picture. I knew I wasn't going to catch trout that trip. Yet I kept thinking, my mind working as it was, that maybe we still might find the trout and it would make a pretty good story, even if I didn't get in the kind of sport I like.

Ten years later, I'm still married to Kay. I think the fact we successfully returned from that trip, at least in regards of getting back alive, is precisely the reason we *are* still married. It's been as difficult as it was those five days. We've spent a lot of time lost, or at least not knowing where we were or where we were going. Things have gotten broken along the way, too—even things that meant a whole lot to one of us and we feel can never be repaired or replaced. There really aren't any trails through a marriage. Even if we had found those trout, there would have been something else outside ourselves that we would have started looking for, thinking it mattered, something we'd never have been able to find.

I kept trying to keep us to higher ground. Yet when Peter and I returned the following year and walked straight to the trout, I discovered they were *below* the meadows from which we initially embarked. So that whole trip with Kay, I kept us banging our heads against the steepest, ruggedest country, thinking *up*, when everything was down.

I still have one more rod to repair. Ed Hartzell in Portland says he can find or fashion me new parts, as he did with the one I rebuilt for Peter. And even if I get into it a little deeper than I can afford these days, my back being what it is, I'm still miles ahead, when you consider the end product and what a new cane rod costs today.

Then it's just a question of giving it to the right person. My eldest son Speed is the obvious choice: he started fishing the fly this year, and even if he is a little young and I don't actually give it to him as his own, he can use it as if it were. Which may be the true spirit of these cane rods: nobody ultimately owns them. I know I can't be trusted.

Building Good Rods Cheap

FROM SEPIC'S JOURNALS

I'm troubled how long this one took. A sign of something: age, attitude, submission to responsibility, perhaps a loss of edge. I recall reaching for the lowest brand of overseas knockoff, $79.99 *including* reel, thinking, *Why not? I can't touch the price, and we're fishing tomorrow. You think Speed will know the difference?*

He wouldn't. Not now, at least. Still, each time I returned the cheap, but perfectly adequate beginner's outfit to the display rack at the local Big 5, I understood I was behaving irrationally, a response to seditious attitudes that would one day subvert all sense of balance in my eldest son's life.

The message was clear: the sport has nothing to do with bottom lines. We're in it for the style, the feeling, the effect, and other spurious notions that translate, in the long haul, to the squirmiest hopes of grace.

I made the call. Finally, I made the call. Jim at the catalogue number took my order. I went round and round about whether or not to buy a kit, weighing options on blanks, reel seats, handle styles, and substitution costs as if shopping for health insurance. At least that's my impression of the process. The next time I have a real job—or any inroads to coverage—I swear I'm going to give equal attention to review of my family health care.

This was no time, you see, for frivolity. I haven't received wages in the three years since I plummeted those twenty-odd feet from a length of dislodged fascia, compressing L1 vertebra as if a chunk of Styrofoam beneath the fall of a hammer. Which to my way of thinking was all the more reason to secure components for the best possible rod I could afford. The next time I light, I might not prove so lucky.

And given one look at my son's first fly rod, the last thing anybody could say about me is that I didn't care. Or provide.

Now, besides materials, the first thing you need if you plan to build yourself or anyone else a fly rod is a favorable work space: somewhere long, flat, and periodically clean, with a modicum of fair lighting, and all your own. In fact, the first thing you need if you don't have this place already in your life is to find and secure it right now.

I mean it. This is serious business. Where else are you going to experiment and create, cogitate or meditate, tie flies, or even tie one on? I sometimes wonder why people provide themselves a bright, clean place to defecate and then do the second or third best thing they love in life in, say, a tiny, dark corner of the garage. You figure it.

Once you've claimed that space, you also need to hold onto it. You may prove your own worst enemy. Before building this last rod, I attended school for a year, as well as taught, and my work space had taken on the aspect of the interior of a high school locker. Occasionally, I shoved debris away from my vise and tied a dozen flies, only to leave behind a new layer of detritus, as though fallout from an abandoned fad. When I finally got around to making room for the arrival of Speed's rod blank, it was like participating in an archeological dig from which I could re-create a time line of the past year's fishing history, sparse though it had been.

Oh, here's that marabou from those damsel nymphs for desert hogs. Okay, now this must be the saddle hackle for San Diego perch streamers. Yeah, and all this lead and black ostrich herl must have been those stone nymphs for the Deschutes ...

What this has to do with rod building is this: that bench or table or sheet of cheap plywood on top of a pair of sawhorses is your commitment to something bigger than yourself, a way of saying that despite anything else coming down the pipe, you aren't rolling onto your back, feet in the air. You build your own rods and you're in the game for keeps. It may be the thing that gets you to the stream.

I chose the kit. An 8-foot for a 4-weight, it promised compatibility with an eleven-year-old in a way I never experienced with hand-me-down production split-cane rods, sought after today like phonographs, muscle cars or, in circles I know of, rayon hosiery. I just considered them fly rods: long, elegant, but unwieldy beasts, practically impossible to cast in the bushwhack drainages in which I began, yet pragmatic as gravity for dapping, dingle fishing, and various other guerrilla tactics employed for presenting the fly in close quarters.

Nobody I knew, however, built such things. Fly rods belonged to that special class of sporting equipment that, like baseball bats and surfboards, appeared simple enough in outline, but possessed an unfathomable architecture that made their creation mysterious, magical, otherworldly. They were objects purchased, not made.

Kits have eliminated much of the mystery—as well as the frustration that often haunts attempts to mix and match disparate components. This was the first kit I ever ordered, and I was grateful for the ease with which the pieces fit, the fact I didn't need to fuss with tip and guide sizes, radical discrepancies between exterior blank diameters and the interiors of the handle and reel seat. Clearly, a degree of fiddling and creative manipulation is expected, if not also desired in the spirit of the work. But for me, there remains a line, however vague, between riding and reinventing the wheel.

What I need to discount is the impression I may be giving that a rod you build is superior to one you buy, or that building your own will make you a better fly fisher. Or person. If we feel any of this is about value or self-worth, we may want to reflect upon our motives for climbing into our waders in the first place.

This will one day be etched in stone, but until then, I feel it worth dogmatic repetition: "Angling," wrote Tom McGuane, "is extremely time consuming. That's sort of the whole point."

The truth is, it wasn't until I began breaking rods that I started building them in earnest. This is no time to go into that— other than to say that the impressive dexterities involved in destroying a fishing rod do not exclude possession of those required to build one, as well. At the risk of debunking prestige, I place the degree of difficulty in rod assembly somewhere between cabinetry and bread making, hanging a front door and making passable love. I leave the criteria up for grabs.

$123.86. The price included shipping and handling, but not thread, glue, epoxy, guide-wrap color preserver, or varnish. This may be as technical as I get: four, six, even eight coats of varnish on your wraps (more coats, now that it's almost all water-based) gives the kind of slow, glassy buildup that the one-shot epoxies can't match. Unless I'm building one rod right after another, I spring for the ounce of fresh, clean varnish. Details don't necessarily catch fish. Or maybe they do, and it starts right here.

Compared with manufactured rods, the kind that you look at when you visit a real shop and think only about yourself, that hundred-and-a-quarter won't buy more than the time of day. I have nothing but good things to say about the business: the marriage between sport and livelihood, between the actual cost of rods and the value we place on them, have as much to do with the nature of things as the cycle of dynamics that spins the snow on the mountains through the surf breaking along my favorite beach. But I will also say this: somewhere it all breaks down if the industry becomes solely extractive, if we think we can buy our way without putting more of ourselves back.

Let me interject another example how it works for me. My father takes a 9-weight surf rod I had just built him from a highly reputable blank and visits a particular retail establishment, a bastion of the industry where no rod under three hundred dollars exists. He's looking for a rod bag. The owner of said establishment checks out the rod, asks who built it, and tells my father I can have a job any day I want.

Fathers fall easily to pride. Mine phones and relates the tale, the glowing compliments regarding the craftsmanship displayed in his new rod, the hint that I might entertain notions of honest-to-God employment.

I hate to shatter others' illusions of myself. My logic, however, is impeccably pure. "They couldn't pay me to build rods for a living."

Still, the question remains: Why? Why build if I can buy? On the other hand, it might be just as valid to ask, Why buy if I can build? Perhaps the point is nothing more than this: building rods for family, friends, or yourself is as much an opportunity as anything else, a chance to explore another aspect of the sphere.

That feels squishy, but such answers often are. I may spin that rod ten thousand times before it's wrapped and on the water. Maybe it's no different than, say, changing diapers for two years: it can't help but make you feel closer.

Speed picked out his own colors. He'd been after me to replicate the Rainbow, a five-weight I wrapped with tailings from leftover spools of thread, none of them sufficient for an entire rod, the sort of vulgar creation you need to get out of your system only once. He settled for baby blue and fire-engine red. For the grip, I had asked that the kit include the slenderest possible Reverse Half Wells. The reel seat that arrived looked to have abetted further depletion of the world's most elegant hardwood rain forests.

One afternoon at the bench, I explained to Speed the mechanics of resins and epoxies, the relation of strength to hardening speed, the reason the reaction gives off heat. I went on and on, at the same time thinking *Here's another gift of the process: making science real for an eleven-year-old.* Then Speed began to fidget.

"You going to do one of those fancy designs above the handle?" he asked.

I understand: my enthusiasm is *not* infectious. Slowly, I have come to sense that my role as a father and teacher may have very little to do with direct instruction, but rather with providing the tools and opportunities for learning, then getting the hell out of the way, so real education can begin.

This doesn't exactly sell at the district level, the capitol, or the local river. And I must confess, from my own schooling, I've any number of bad habits I developed behind the bushes that still provoke distrust in situations demanding delicate presentation.

But I have also learned the lesson that nothing in fly fishing that really matters reflects the judgments of others: what I can do in the way of finding and fooling fish, casting and tying flies, building sound, functional rods and embellishing them with "those fancy designs above the handle" is nothing more, or less, than a measure of time spent how I wish to spend it, the value of which may ultimately have no more meaning than what I pass along, how I help others make time for the path of their own choosing.

The World's Ugliest Fly

FROM SEPIC'S JOURNALS

"What's that?"

"What?"

"*This.*"

*M*c's hand hesitates above the debris atop the motor well: gas receipts, spare change, hand tools—that bobber found along the McKenzie with the Mepps spinner still affixed to it—all of it imbued with the fine patina of dog hair congealed in evaporated black coffee.

"?"

"*This!*"

He tries again, his fingers extending toward the molded cup recess: the pit of eternal filth. I consider mentioning that at least I no longer smoke. But Mc does—which is maybe why he is able to reach in and pluck out the fly, although I do notice he holds it as though it might be . . . .

"Oh, my WUF." I steer the van clear of the edge of the road. "I've been *looking* for that."

"Gray or Grizzly?" Dave lifts the fly to the light of the windshield, turns it side to side in confusion. Insectile? Rodentile? Fecal? "Where're the wings?"

"Not 'Wulff.' . . . *WUF*. Like a dog says—if you asked what's on top of his doghouse."

It's Mc's turn to look dumbly at me. Perhaps it was that asthma prescription when I was a child. I aim the van down the center of the highway, reach, and take the fly. Just holding it, it's hard not to feel, well, flattered.

"WUF?"

I nod, inspecting my handiwork. Pinching the plump, segmented body, I produce a droplet of coffee sputum. It dangles from the hook bend, detaches as if from an infant's chin.

"Never heard of it." Mc crinkles his nose. Maybe the cigarettes still haven't ruined it. When I jab the fly at him, he leans away like a child from a photo of a cobra.

"'Course not. It's one of a kind."

Mc tries. . . . But by the time his hand comes up, I've wrapped the fly in mine, snatched my fist away.

"One of *what* kind?"

Like a nugget in a miner's pan, the grub lay nestled in the weeping debris captured by the river screen, a dollop of pure protein that would make any trout's heart sing. In size approximately the top inch of a pencil, the head, although dark, similarly proportioned to a well-used eraser, the creature appeared to be a member of the *Ticonderoga* genus, perhaps a medium-lead number 2. (I admit some confusion with the finer points of aquatic entomology, especially with regard to these early larval stages. Frankly, I thought for a moment I may well be gazing at an example of *T. cervix vulgaris*—the redoubtable Pencil-Neck Geek.) Body color, however, distinguished the plump morsel as exceptional fare. The shade, although again from the pencil end of the spectrum, was more reminiscent of the alluring yellow found in a certain style kitchen of thirty years past, in quiche pans shoved to the back of the refrigerator or, occasionally, the legal-pad hues discovered within the folds of a freshly employed handkerchief. Which is to say, from a trout's point of view, it was a color that looked good enough to eat.

I'm hesitant to divulge secrets. Although it is not one of my dire aspirations, I suspect this pattern may eventually lead to a contract with Umpqua Feather Merchants. Until then, I need to be somewhat cautious. Granted, nothing can prevent knockoffs, and it's easy to envision a day when you walk into shops anywhere and, *bingo*, there it be. Without the trademarked name, however, you'd be advised to question the authenticity of somebody else's World's Ugliest Fly.

It's a matter of principle—as well as, in most cases, food on the fly designer's table. Let's say this first one becomes the "World" series: you know, change a little this, tweak it a little there. *Regionalize.* Not that I could delude myself with thoughts of ever approaching, oh, the *ten thousand dozen* sales figure reached last year by Mr. Whitlock's hopper pattern. Not even by calculations of 10 percent. Wholesale, that is.

I hope I don't give the impression I'm plagued by greed, paranoia, or questions of self-esteem. It's just that some of my vise tactics and streamside strategies are not yet so honed that I feel they're ready for any but the most discerning audience. I phoned Andy Burk to solicit his take on contract fly designs, and he made the observation that no matter how good you are, "you can bet there's some kid out back in a shed in Pennsylvania who's doing something new and better than the rest of us are." Which is easy to say when you've made a name for yourself surrounded by pretty damsels. And, anyway, it's the thirteen-year-old in Downey that makes *me* cringe.

Naturally, I'm trying to free myself from these sorts of limiting thoughts. Because I know that each one of us has something special to share. Having fished solely with me throughout their entire lives, for example, my sons have learned that a good day of fishing does not necessarily have anything to do with how many fish are caught. In fact, with me as their mentor, they both currently hold the firm belief that fishing has nothing to do with catching fish at all.

My hook of choice was the old Mustad 37160 wide-gape English bait design, which nobody recommends anymore because of its tendency, in the larger sizes, to hook fish through the eye and brain. Personally, I'm ambivalent about the matter. It assumes a fish actually will be fooled by the fly in the first place. I know we're told these days to visualize success, that we can't expect our dreams to come true unless we expect our dreams to come true. But some of us choose fishing to escape this sort of morbid logic from the start.

I didn't, of course, intend it be the World's Ugliest Fly. I mean, I know there isn't anything in nature inherently ugly—certainly nothing on which a trout feeds, which helps us see beauty in any number of equivocal guises. Carry that thinking far enough and you can wrap the Big Picture in divinity. I do it all the time. Yet it is the absurd artificiality of sport that propels us from mere imitative thoughts to ones of true creativity. The hologram includes us! The world of the trout is perfect without the human species, but ours would be incomplete—and sorry indeed—without the trout. The insinuation is that despite our misdeeds, we actually belong. More fabulous still is the recognition of that self-same notion through the window made available to us from, among other vantage points, the ingenuous perspective of fly fishing.

I would have preferred not to weight it. In my fantasy world, trout would have built-in blinders and eyeball-pivot reducers that restrict their vision to the upper quadrant of the optic field. Anything below their lateral lines would be ignored. In this case, trout also would be as thin as clothespins, and a big one maybe four inches long. So I accept the trade-off and wrap lead on the hooks of my big nymphs. I still haven't come to peace with split shot and strike indicators, but only because my trout experience is relatively limited, and in the surf, where fish occupy far less specific confines, adroit casting remains eminently important.

Still, you can do a lot with lead. I'm particularly impressed by the practice of using a plump, severely weighted nymph to sink a second, smaller and less, shall we say, intrusive fly. It reminds me how we used to rig a pyramid sinker beneath our sand crabs while perch fishing. I heard Seth Norman talk once about using a sixteen-ounce lead ball to get his fly down to Golden Gate salmon for completion of a difficult story assignment, a back-alley tactic he felt reasonably settled with by filing it under the concept of the All-Synthetic Fly. But clearly, I was dealing here with a fat, juicy grub I would want to tumble along the bottom, so lead it was—for profile, weight, and the off chance I would need to regain the streamside attention of Lucy, my retriever, through the dimensions of her anvilesque skull, thickened over two hundred years of selective breeding.

The rest of the fly went together like a dream. That is, it looks like I tied it while asleep.

Only a select few patterns are truly unique. When Dan Blanton, for instance, first tied his saltwater Whistler, thirty-plus years ago and counting, there just wasn't anything else like it. Now you see Whistlers everywhere—although they're not all called that. On the other hand, some that *are* called Whistlers aren't true to Blanton's own design. It can get messy. What is original? What is new? Listening to a Dan Blanton talk on the subject, one of his favorites, you hear phrases like "bonafide new pattern . . . not a variation of an existing . . . slight change . . . fly plagiarism." The basis of his authority, as far as I'm concerned, is a fly like a Whistler that appears on the scene without prece-dent—more of a sudden mutation than an obvious step of evolu-tion. Of course, the perspective of time will always separate the innovators from the imitators. A fly such as Dan Blanton's Whistler was a start. Then everybody else goes from there.

Now, the problem with truly creative fly design is the ratio between success and failure. For some, in fact, the question is actually this: What do you really want to do—catch fish, or be famous? You'd be surprised the number of people who have trouble answering that. Or maybe you wouldn't. We all know, deep down, that the old patterns work just fine. But complacency does not produce the likes of a World's Ugliest Fly.

My father would call it a one-off. He's been in charge of building everything from internal insulin dispensers to turbine engines for the MX missile. The one-off is not so much a prototype as it is a true, one-of-a-kind product. The Spruce Goose was a one-off. So are lots of surfboards, cane rods, wooden boats, and even pieces of farm equipment. To build a one-off is to declare: "Hey, this is how I want it. This is what I want it to look like and do."

Ever since John Gierach related A. K. Best's "100-dozen" measure for getting to know a pattern, a lot of us plebeian tiers have felt, well, ashamed for our lack of order, discipline, and gross output. We're practically always tying one-offs. Of course, some of us try to argue that this leaves room for divine inspiration, the stroke of genius, a bolt from the blue, or, in rare cases, from a bottle. Which is precisely how you stumble upon a fly like the World's Ugliest.

I guess a big part of the difference is what you get from being an amateur with an avocation, as opposed to a professional with a job. The particular fly in question would pencil-out to sell for about, say, $8.95.

So here's where the contract comes in. You got it right, you got something special, something unique, one of a kind. Now let's crank these babies out. The challenge for a company like Umpqua Feather Merchants is to mass-produce flies that are true to the original design. The consumer of a trademarked pattern should be confident that the fly he or she is buying looks exactly as the designer whose name is affixed to it intended. Quality control is everything. Whether or not the angler is also buying into a system exploiting cheap overseas labor is a question of moral latitudes I don't feel capable of exploring, deferring, in this instance, to more incendiary minds and opinions of greater hubris.

The success of the contract company in accurately replicating a particular pattern is judged differently by different tiers/designers. Now I'm getting personal. Let's just say that one tier I talked to asserts that random samples sent to him by Umpqua are "all over the board," while another claims some of the flies he receives look "just like I tied them myself." Ken Menard, new-products manager at Umpqua, says that certain tiers simply stay more involved with the process than others. "You get guys who pay a lot of attention to the samples. Others are pretty laissez-faire." I guess it's safe to say that, as usual, opinions vary.

Of course, I personally wouldn't expect the production of the World's Ugliest Fly to include repeated dunkings into large vats of tepid coffee. Then again, this or some similar step may prove crucial to the fly's ultimate effectiveness. Because the question remains: How ugly is it?

Certainly, I've tied plenty of competitors. Like tattoos, paisley shirts, and bad marriages, this kind of fly never seems to go away. They turn up everywhere. Who's got the heart to throw them out? *You just never know*, you tell yourself, as though you may stumble upon a hatch in the wastewater below the neighborhood reactor. Evolution can take the strangest of turns. You're ready . . . if the picture goes absolutely haywire.

Still, everybody you talk to agrees that the number-one criterion for any new fly to make its way in this world is whether or not it works. Does it catch fish? You would think here, at least, we're finally dealing with a relatively straightforward question. I mean, *does it catch fish?*

Let me try to put that question into perspective. Besides the

World's Ugliest, there's another fly of mine you may eventually see or hear about. I call it the Thermos. The name comes from the story about the guy who believes this particular invention is man's greatest ever because it keeps hot things hot and cold things cold.

"How do it know?" he asks.

You see, I've got a lot of Thermos flies—that is, flies that have never touched the water, and thus, obviously, have never caught a fish. But who's to say they wouldn't? Even the World's Ugliest may prove itself as good as any—a fly that catches fish when you fish it, doesn't when you don't. How do it know?

Lucy
FROM SEPIC'S JOURNALS

*L*ike most dedicated fly fishers, I read too much. Worse, I generally believe what I read. So when I moved to the Northwest after years of digesting the works of Roderick Haig-Brown, my inclination was to get myself a fishing dog. I especially liked the image of me fighting fearless steelhead, sex-inflamed salmon, or, say, mere three-pound sea-run cutthroats, my riverwise retriever waiting patiently on the bank, only to glide out into the margins of the brawling current to secure yet another trophy, then gently deposit it where we might indulge a moment in shared glory, the manifold blessings that brought this instant to be, before returning the fish to its fated journey within the great and gracious stream of life.

In other words, I suffered the lowest form of self-deceit, as spurious in every detail as my hand-to-mouth images of marriage, fatherhood, or country gentility. A fishing dog? I might as well have ordered love sonnets out of the barrel of a riot gun.

This is one way this kind of thing can happen. Kay and I sit at opposite ends of a powder-blue leather couch, expressing differences of opinion. It is called "expressing" because of the presence of a counselor to whom we will soon write a check. At home, it is free of charge and called "fighting." I remain troubled by the direction of some of Kay's e-mail correspondence. She feels I am stifling a wave of unprecedented creativity in her life. This is right up there with financial authority, in-laws, and contraception.

We all know, of course, what the *real* issue is. For some strange reason, however, our discord has focused upon the topic of getting a dog. Kay believes it will be good for me. I'm thinking it's one more thing in my life, despite my literature-induced predilections. I'm also still working for the slash-and-burn contractor at the time, so my general impression of circumstances is that of the one-armed wallpaper hanger. Plus, I've yet to convince myself, all things considered, that I can care adequately for my own two sons.

And then there's the matter of the last dog I owned. His name was George. He was a Dalmatian without papers, probably due to the bad gene that produced dimensions double the breed standard. He might also have been disqualified on grounds of sexual precocity. I was sixteen, and thus unreliable in the appraisal of such matters. The notion of a "two-peckered billy goat" had yet to crystallize in my personal imagery. But it was clear from the start that I was in over my head.

Now that I think about it, I probably got George for the same reason Kay began suggesting I get a dog. It was said it would be good for me. I look at that reasoning now and consider similar arguments in favor of brewer's yeast, abstinence, and corporal punishment. I believe in my right to be gun-shy.

Poor George. He was relegated to the side yard, that special purgatory of classic suburban abuse. God forbid he should run free around the swimming pool. We descended into the worst sort of codependency. I wanted a dog, but I didn't want *this*. George responded to obedience training with tantrums and greetings of carnal deviancy. I had one friend, Craig Epstein, who stopped visiting, he was so humiliated. The depth of our communication settled at the level of heavy shank bones I retrieved each week from the meat market where I held a Saturday job. At best, George understood my hopeless need to please, securing these skeletal offerings crosswise in his teeth, then prancing about his pen as if as a kind of spotted, Paleolithic apparition.

I was attempting to fit George into a typical teenager's schedule of scholastics, after-school sports, socializing, and hormonal angst. Which left about twenty-seven minutes a day. George spent the rest of time begging for attention. Or plotting revenge.

The crisis condition developed around George's ability to whine mercilessly at all hours of the night directly outside my parents' bedroom window. George had what it takes to keep it up. It's impossible to know whether or not he actually *intended* to undermine the sanity of the household. Breakfasts became a painful ordeal as my father—already taxed by professional aspirations, torturous freeway commutes, and, well, fatherhood—seized the problem in his mind's direct, bass-busting ways. I remember one morning having difficulty swallowing my orange juice and thinking, *Somebody's going to get hurt here.*

One night, George did. Shortly afterward, my mother took him to an animal shelter, leaving him chained outside the gate. The facility was already filled beyond capacity with other dogs discarded by people who should have never owned one in the first place. Which is the same sad road Lucy was headed down until I fell and broke my back.

Chesapeake owners like to recount the tale of the legendary progenitors of the breed, a pair of Newfoundland puppies rescued from a shipwreck in 1807. The listener is meant to understand that these Romantic beginnings foretold a certain heartiness of spirit, if not also evidence of spontaneous, divine approval. John Gierach writes about a Montana friend's Chessie, famous for both heroic retrieves and the unnerving habit of occasionally devouring the kill. I told Kay this story and she agreed: "*That's* Lucy!"

Kay has had her own impressions of Lucy all along. She presumes, for one, that she should be able to pet such a sweet-faced creature without detonating attempts at full-scale ascendancy. Naturally, this belief sheds a certain light my way, whence I'm called upon to intervene. My own impression of Lucy in these scenes is the cartoon imagery of an overheating thermometer, the red mercury rising swiftly through the stem, the glass filling and swelling and pulsing, drawing us forward to the edge of our seats until the sudden, fateful explosion. Often, I'm moved to suggest to Kay she contain her own affections.

"Why even have a dog if you can't pet her?" Why indeed? Well, Lucy, I'm reminded, has been good for me.

We bought her from a breeder out past Camas, Washington, another California transplant with acreage, horses, a pole barn, and redneck convictions. Maybe it was all those years adjusting claims in the South Bay or San Fernando Valley. These guys have become fixtures throughout the rural Northwest, bringing with them the hostility of a Friday freeway commute. I don't know what that makes me. Probably the flip side of the same coin.

I got the pick of the litter. Which is to say, I chose the one the color I liked. Then I asked for help verifying its sex. She was three weeks old, and I tried to begin imagining a deepening connection. As advised by the breeder, I also marked her with pink nail polish to be certain of her identity when I returned to separate her from her mother. I asked the breeder's daughter to begin calling her "Lucy."

I remember shortly before Speed was born how it suddenly occurred to me one day that we needed to get ready. I had built a cradle months before, then suffered a dissociation with the outcome of Kay's advancing pregnancy. You can live in the moment, but this was another thing altogether. So maybe I shouldn't be surprised that the only preparations I made for Lucy was to buy a bag of puppy chow and clear out a corner of the garage.

On the other hand, I've become certain through the years that most of us wouldn't do much anything of real interest if we waited to start until we had our lives perfectly in order. I mean, as the reverend said, you want to make God laugh, tell Him your plans.

Still, it was a lonely first winter for Lucy. Time was already spread thin, and I was convinced my life would improve only if others changed, that perverse delusion of victimhood for which my marriage and job seemed to the perfect role models. Worse, when I did find a moment or two for Lucy, I adopted a hard-nosed attitude on the assumption that submission was the ultimate goal. Even the vet and puppy obedience school trainer advised me to be firm. "You've got to stop her from being *that* way!" they warned me again and again.

But all Lucy really wanted was to be part of the family. One day, I concluded I didn't like working twelve hours a day for a contractor who burned up both his subs and his employees, no matter what the money, and that was that. I drove home and opened the garage. Lucy came out like a Skilsaw in a nightmare, yet as I watched her tear around the yard and leap directly into my face, I saw that she acted like a good fish when hooked, springing wildly as if on top of the water. I snapped the leash on her and let her drag me to the street. At six months, she was maybe sixty-five pounds, but she played, as they say, bigger. We walked to the woods, an undeveloped city park beyond the dead end, and once in the trees, I had her sit and stay. I unfastened her and moved farther down the trail. Lucy sat there obediently, intent as an umpire, her muscles visibly quivering. Finally I called her to come, which she did, blowing by me and deeper into the woods.

It was early March, the trees just beginning to leaf, the shock of trilliums sprinkled here and there in the sodden winter debris. Lucy bolted back up the path, spinning round me and off again. In contrast to all of our other problems, she had a comfort level at the edge of sight, which she never overshot. I caught up with her down in the hollow and swale, the water about normal for the time of year. Lucy raced splashing up and down the creek, bounding like a deer trapped by fire.

But then birds grew used to us and began appearing—first the little winter wrens flitting about, then the towhees and thrushes and robins. A wave of bushtits blew through a big maple directly above, leaving behind a pair of juncos, a single yellow-crowned kinglet. *This is impossibly fucking nice*, I thought: *a dog in the woods, birds in the trees.* Atop a riddled snag, a pili-ated woodpecker started pounding, below it a carpenter's circle of chips and shavings. I was reminded I didn't have a job.

Lucy returned and thrust her muddy paws on me, her yellow eyes searching mine. I let her do everything she wasn't supposed to, begging her forgiveness. How else could I forgive myself? We stood there, well, come on—dancing!—her tail going crazy, the outlandish tip of the iceberg of those nearly two centuries of selective breeding. It wasn't quite a commitment to do whatever it takes—a decision I hadn't even reached as a father or a hus-band—but for the first time, I saw through to Lucy, an image of myself and my hopeless need for love.

There was a moment during Lucy's first month home that says it all. She pranced into the kitchen and raised her nose to fur-ther her acquaintance with the cat upon the chair. Phoebe, one of those small, cautious females deadly on the prowl, looked calmly down at Lucy's wide-eyed excitement, then aimed and opened a slit in my three-hundred-dollar puppy's amber eyeball. And this is how it can be: wonder becomes the only appropriate response to the mysteries of give and take. We are all inevitably hurt and sometimes scarred. But a dog can teach us, if we allow it to, what we refuse to learn elsewhere or alone. What *had* I been afraid of up to now?

This is another way it can be. There's a big eddy in the stretch of the Deschutes I've been fishing since I got here, one that holds innumerable large trout that feed most evenings like cavorting porpoises. There are similar spots all up and down the river, some of them lined up one after the other, so where I'm talking about doesn't exactly matter. This just happens to be the first place I stumbled upon, and from it I'm determined, eventually, to catch a humongous trout. I haven't yet.

The way I figure it, I need to catch a big fish *there* in order to claim I've learned something. Any other spot might just mean a small, stupid trout, a lucky drift, or another mistake by that big guy known by every other angler as Old Dead Eye. I know it doesn't really make sense, but what else can I say? I've wasted *days* there.

So when my buddy Peter came up to fish the North Fork after I broke my back, I decided we should fish that big eddy on our way back to PDX. Peter's brother John was also along, having driven up from the Bay Area. Several days on the North Fork had produced lots of fun, lots of fish, but only the one trout of any size, a rainbow that exploded under the biggest dry fly I've ever used. I figured I owed it to Peter to at least show him some real fish. I believe we would both agree, however, that being led to fish that one can necessarily catch is really far too much to ask of a friend.

Now, asking him to leave his dog home might be another thing altogether. It wasn't as bad as it might have been. Come sunset, everything went as expected: the rise, the refusals, the awestruck moaning and groaning as eight, nine, ten—how many?—inches showed between the ghostly appearance and disappearance of porpoising dorsal and caudal fins. We were all fishing our own vague interpretations of the tiniest of emergers on ungodly long light leaders, all with equal degrees of success, or lack of it . . . until Peter hooked up!

The fish swam directly for a snag in the middle of the eddy, took one complete turn around it, and broke the leader. It wasn't even a contest. I think they learn that one before they're allowed into the heart of the eddy. Sort of like it used to be with parallel parking before you could get your driver's license.

Anyway, it was all but dark by then, and I figured Peter wouldn't have enough light to tie on another fly. I had been fishing just above the eddy, a weird little drift disturbed by yet more big, smart trout that I hadn't fooled, while holding Lucy on the leash at my side. I let her free. I knew she would immediately hit the water—nearly two centuries of breeding and counting!—but I felt there was plenty of room between me and my guests, even if they were fishing blind.

When Kay said "*That's* Lucy!" this is what she meant: rather than enter the river in front of me, Lucy headed straight for Peter and John and leaped into the water directly between them. She swam out the distance of their casts, then turned and looked back at them. Then she began splashing, trying to bite the water, and barking all at the same time. Up until then, Peter and John had again been fishing.

It's hard to argue willful intent. Love, I think, is as much an instinct as hunger, fear, or the zeal for reproduction. That trout in the big eddy didn't treat Peter with disdain for personal reasons. Lucy, I believe, reflects that pure survival mechanism we equate with the heart. She knows where to get attention, and how.

I returned home from that trip and, despite my back, built Lucy a kennel, a doghouse, and fenced in the entire backyard. I continued to take her fishing, and she now joins me pretty much wherever I go, riding shotgun in the van, hanging out with me in the garage and basement office.

I wish that I could report that Lacy has become the dog I often read about and imagined on the water as my own. We're still working on it. Occasionally, I get so angry, hollering like an old fart who just had his flower bed trampled, that she leaves the stream and trots disdainfully back to camp. But she generally doesn't give up that easily. Sometimes, now, I don't even try to restrain or discipline her, entertaining the notion that the only way our relationship will work is if Lucy understands the goal of the sport and *chooses* to behave with quiet patience in accordance with the common good. Perhaps the problem is that she's still waiting for *me* to hook those good fish, so she can pounce into the river and ferry them to my side.

Desert Pigs
From Sepic's Journals

*M*c didn't want the boys to come—a surprise, because he's usually receptive to the idea. He knows, for one, it's either that, or there's a good chance I'm not going fishing anyway.

"It's my *bachelor* party," he argued. "I don't think *you'd* want them along."

Okay. But maybe I wouldn't belong, either. I mean, a man of my age. I suffered an image of the female torso delineated by peripheries of hip waders and the new Orvis Easy Entry Vest. Somehow, this brought to mind how much I still dislike taking part in tying circles, the exposure of my inability to execute an effortless whip finish. And all those vials around. No telling what's in fashion, these days. Exactly what kind of lake was this anyway?

"Just some ponds some guy dug out in the middle of nowhere. Would remind you of water at a golf course—without the golf course!" I heard Mc chuckle, amused by the accuracy of his own imagery. Had the party started already?

We worked out the details: where we'd meet, when, who was driving. My friendship with Mc, though new, had crystallized upon his introducing me to the North Fork. I knew he could be trusted, that we were both looking for close enough to the same things in fishing that our differences would never amount to much. Still: *a bachelor party?*

I held the phone between shoulder and ear, trying to follow the route in my new *DeLorme Oregon Atlas & Gazetteer*. And as the green pages of mountains and forests gave way to the empty white of badland desert, I began to feel a familiar tingle, recognize the spirit of our destination. Hey, I'd been here before. Not the same place, not exactly, no. But near enough I knew what was coming.

"You say you got fish there last time?"

Mc explained how he would soon be related through his wife to the fellow whose own bachelor party at the lake he had attended the year before. Then he said no, he had *hooked* fish there.

"What does *that* mean?" I asked.

"Means I hooked fish. And then I held on and went along for the ride."

Now, I hate that kind of talk. It's the oldest come-on in the literature: *The Place Where Nobody Landed a Fish!* My own descent into temptation includes the very same obscenities, which I neglect to mention to the therapists on the grounds that I always refrain, in my version of the story, to claim I then showed up and "whipped a mother." Nevertheless, like the classic soft-hackle wet fly, the reason the ploy has been used for centuries is that it works. I could hardly wait for more?

"How many fish did you catch, Mc?"

"Oh, I must've hooked four, five, maybe—"

"How many did you *catch*, Mc? You know: land, net, beach?"

"None. Not one."

"Hmm."

I can't help it. If I were a fish, I'd be somebody's memory. Or the one with the pattern of piercings ornamenting its lips.

"'Kind of fish were they, Mc? What kind of fish were these you hooked and rode and didn't land?"

"Hogs," Mc answered. "Great big ol' hogs."

"Thought so."

Being from California, I know a little bit about big desert trout. Being from California, I might also contend I know a little bit about everything. But I won't. And I certainly can't argue that more than three decades of fishing for hatchery-produced rainbows—that is, synthetic trout dumped into the elaborately engineered holdings of what Wallace Stegner called the world's most massive "oasis civilization" and there grown to obscene proportions on the potency of year-round arid-lands sunshine—I can't argue that this kind of fishery taught me much of anything I think I need to know as a fly fisherman, a sportsman, a citizen of the West, or even a human being. But I do think it taught me something.

Let's start with this: the widespread proliferation of trophy trout fisheries throughout much of the arid West embraces deeply rooted environmental dangers now threatening the health and welfare of entire watersheds and native wildlife alike. Or how about this: put-and-take arid-lands trout fishing accelerates the moral, ethical, aesthetic, and spiritual degradation of vast numbers of Western anglers.

Or even this: catch-and-release fishing—as now practiced by most serious fly fishers—inspires wholesale levels of greed, covetousness, and lust, producing modern anglers who often are no longer attempting to insinuate themselves into the natural scheme and rhythm of things, but instead are *competing* with their fellow anglers via an increasing reliance on aspects of the sport that are technical, rather than intuitive, spontaneous, or simply creative.

Then again, what but hardy rainbows grow better in the brilliant sunshine and clean, cool water captured at the margins and precipice of humanity's inviolate needs?

We arrived at the locked gate to the lakes under high, paisley skies scoured by the sort of late-afternoon badland wind that brings to mind Nevada, western Wyoming, or even the

Pacific coast of Baja. I knew I'd been somewhere like this before. It was all semidesert rangeland—sage, coulees, and abrupt, layered geology—and clumped together in the distance where you knew there were springs stood an assortment of young trees and a log cabin, the rental of which provided sole access to the water. We could also see vehicles there. The group ahead of us rightfully had the lakes until the following morning. But the wind was just nasty enough that we figured they might cut their stay short.

Our own group turned out to include a grand total of four. I began to sense this really might be about fishing, after all. Jack Newton had followed us over in his own truck from the valley, and waiting for us alongside the cabin was another of Mc's old college pals, Rob Bullis, from Bend, who had arranged the same kind of party the year before after fishing the lakes with guides on their days off—always a good recommendation.

Sure enough, by the time I was introduced all around, guys from the group ahead of us were straggling in from the lakes, breaking down rods and loading gear from the cabin, the mood not exactly what I would call elated as the wind throttled up and down somewhere between hoot and honk.

Mc again impressed me with his usual goodwill when he stated to nobody in particular, "At least there's some cloud cover!" A guy leaving looked over at us like we'd just tossed him a bone. The four of us all gazed up through the wind, nodding in agreement about the existence of some cloud cover. And shortly after the group drove off, leaving us with the place to ourselves, Rob offered the sort of observation that made me see right off why he was Mc's friend, and why I would probably get along with him, too.

"They 'got a couple' means they saw 'em and that's it. Then this wind started blowing."

Mc and I went for a stroll anyway—just, you know, to look around. It really was an impossible blow. We didn't even carry rods. We followed a trail out over patches of marsh outlined by contours of alkaline precipitates, finally coming to a small wooden footbridge built across a narrow ditchlike inlet that ran directly from a spring into one of the lakes. Mc was right: it all did remind you of water at a golf course. I was just about to make a comment about the difficulty of club selection in this kind of wind when Mc stopped short, thrusting his arm out in front of me like a referee.

"There!" he whispered. "See it?"

Now, in this situation you've got a few different options. I no longer entertain intimations of doom. My very oldest recurring nightmare involves arriving at just the right moment at some terrific fishing or surfing spot and then failing to get it together to enjoy the action. Usually, darkness is descending, and the last hour of sport grows dim. I'm witness to perfect waves spinning down the beach or point, guys getting outlandish rides or deep, deep barrels, or there are signs of fish everywhere, boils or rolls, birds feeding, at least somebody somewhere has one on or just did and is now showing me a brilliant fish I feel like I would die for. Then the trouble begins. Everything starts to go wrong. I stand out maybe knee-deep in water, only to have the fin of my board fall off, or there's no reel on my rod, or I can't tie a knot, my flies are all raisins, my board is now a tennis racket, or the truck is floating through the pool and *what the hell am I going to do!*

But as I said, I don't allow that kind of thinking to get the best of me anymore. I'm here to tell you there's hope on every horizon! I stood there beside Mc, breathing as quietly as I could, trying to melt into the sage. The cast would have been improbable on the calmest of days, the inlet too narrow for anything but dapping, nearly too small for the big trout itself. I eased backward, breath by breath, the wind stinging my wide-open eyes.

"Well, maybe if you cast at just the right angle, you could at least get a fly, you know, on the water." I didn't hear if Mc agreed with me or not as I turned toward the cabin, breaking into a dead run.

But I still find this kind of fishing troublesome. It's not that I think it wrong, or inane, or morally decrepit—or even the kind of sport I wouldn't want to introduce to my sons. I won't even contend that I don't like it. Lord knows, the last thing we need more of in this world is judgment and condemnation. But the thing is this: as long as we accept these man-made trout grotesqueries as a substitute for fishing in naturally sustained, healthy rivers, lakes, and streams, we're on our way to consenting to the sort of enervated, second-rate citizenry that turns anglers into little more than recreational users, quick-fix junkies, and compulsive, shopping-mall consumers. All of whom I recognize at times as myself.

Silver Lake did include a golf course. Also the requisite clubhouse, 10,000-square-foot building lots, an equestrian park, and a distinct impression of resale potential—all within a mere hour's commute to the edge of the greater L.A. basin. This would have been sometime before video arcades, aerobics, or anything resembling what is recognizable today as Palmdale or Lancaster. Still, it was obvious somebody had gone to great lengths to create this opportunity for an excellent return on investment, boring down to tap the underground reaches of the Mojave River, bringing water to the light of desert sunshine in that uniquely Southlandish equation for squeezing money out of sand.

Timing was a big part of that equation—even bigger than the golf, though there was an enormous appeal to all that fresh, green grass draped across the otherwise forbidding landscape. And despite the fact the course also had somebody's famous name attached to its design, this was about coming aboard at the right moment, not the sort of financial decision into which the ego should play. My father had always loved his golf, but he calculated risk in an economy of capital and time, not in terms of his handicap, so that even after enjoying a round one Saturday at the Silver Lake, he based his decision to buy a lot on the hard, cold numbers. For him, those numbers just happened to include the half-dozen rainbow trout we saw displayed that afternoon in the clubhouse, fish of four and five pounds laid out like magnums of champagne on cube ice inside an open, Styrofoam cooler.

It will always seem to me that I was somehow on the outside of that party with Mc and his two buddies. There was the age difference, for one, as well as their similar tastes in, well, whatever they may have been tasting in honor of Mc's final hours of bachelorhood. I've been on the inside often enough, sometimes all by myself, like on that trip, say, up in Ontario right after college to a fly-in northern pike lake with my father. *Why all these pictures of mushrooms?* How can you possibly explain?

Yet it's sad to think we are any of us in on this alone The point feels more and more like we should work at it together. My secrets don't make me better—or worse!—than anyone else. My lust has gotten the best of me, but I don't feel fundamentally damaged. On the other hand, I do know I've reached the stage where I need to watch my step.

Mc strolled up out of the twilight through the wind and asked what the hell I was doing. I finished reeling in my line, and when I held the leader up to the glaze of the Western sky, I was surprised to see I still had on the tiny size-20 Beadhead Serendipity. It could have just as easily gone the other way.

"Big trout," I said, redoing my knot while I still had the light. "I had to kind of lean on him when he got out there near that snag."

"Big fucking pigs," said Mc, throwing his backcast straight up, trying to kite his fly out onto the water. "I *thought* I saw you go for a ride."

My father finally got Grandpa to join us one Saturday at Silver

Lake. By now, my grandfather's fishing was entirely geared toward this kind of sport. Yet he had his routine, places of his own, his cronies. They knew about stocking schedules, new openings or reopenings, lakes that hadn't been fished before, or for years, or where a hundred brood-stock fish had just been released. And they knew how to catch these fish, their tactics a textbook agglomeration of Southland reservoir techniques and all the subtleties available in the employment of Kraft marshmallows, Velveeta cheese, Pautzke's salmon eggs, and the like.

I don't want to sound like a smart-ass: my grandfather and his pals knew how to catch the fish they went fishing for—simple as that. They had everything just so, from the way they prepared and carried their bait, the arrangement of pretied swivels and treble hooks so that time was never wasted after getting hung up, and the perfect running condition of small outboards they brought along to use with the lakes' rented boats. And all of these old-timers—but especially Grandpa—had these snazzy little spinning outfits, rods of the proverbial buggy-whip nature and reels that brought to mind something on the order of a cross between a Swiss watch and a doll-sized sewing machine—with the price tags to match.

Still, it took awhile before Grandpa agreed to ride with us out to the desert. Certainly, he wasn't a fan of that kind of heat or sun. And though he hadn't smoked since I was a child, he always spoke with concern about any destination outside the basin proper, reminding us of his troubles breathing at altitudes. But when it gets right down to it, I think the reason my grandfather wasn't all that jazzed over our invitations to Silver Lake was that he simply wasn't impressed by our tales of big fish. He knew what big trout were really about—and they weren't the little cookie-cutter "catchable rainbows" that most reservoir anglers snorted about.

But blood runs as thick in my family as any. Grandpa consented, right down to bringing the lunch, as well as the arsenal of processed baits. He was an old fisherman, and both my father and I had learned from him about listening and doing as we were told. Given that this was the game he now played, Grandpa took charge, accepting responsibility as much as any angler can for the accomplishment of the one goal we shared on such outings: catching fish . . . despite the fact that we had caught plenty of big fish there at Silver Lake on our own.

Now, this is all way down deep in the webby recesses of my fissured memory store. I mean to say, I've been between here and there on roads I don't commend, and precision recall is not apt to show up at this late date. But there was a moment that day that bleeds throughout my mind, and I know it came after my father got into a fish that gave him undue trouble because it was foul-hooked, a fairly typical Silver Lake rainbow that fought for a long time a hundred yards off the bow of the boat, out near a tie-up buoy, and then finally more or less rolled over and died, so that my father still had a hard time bringing it to the net, drawing it broadside through the surface as if his line were affixed midlength to a waterlogged chunk of two-by-four.

Grandpa gave my father a going-over about that fish. Foul-hooked or not, he insinuated, the fish wasn't so big my father should have had to kill it just to bring it to the boat. Naturally, the needle wasn't pointed solely in the direction of questions regarding my father's fishing skills. It was also understood that the trout's life could have been spared had my father been fishing with the sort of sophisticated gear that Grandpa employed.

Don't get me wrong: it wasn't the poor, dumb trout's life that was at issue. This was about being a good fisherman—which in our family was as close as any of the three of us ever got to talking intimately about being a good man.

Then Grandpa hooked a fish, came up tight on it with his fine-tuned gear, the little reel humming in his still-powerful tradesman hands, and all of sudden, his rod broke. I mean just like that, his rod broke.

My father still talks about it, how at that moment he thought Grandpa was going to cry. I don't even know if we tried landing the fish. Grandpa's rod was broken, and though there was at least one other one along with us in the boat, he refused to keep fishing. *His rod was broken!* And he'd be damned if he was going to fish with anybody else's—even if it was one of his own—especially for this kind of trout at this lake, where he didn't even really want to come fishing in the first place. It was as if there was something wrong with the fish. We motored in and drove home.

Mc got a fish to rise to a tiny dry he was dancing off the crests of the chop, just close enough to where I had hooked mine that I thought for an instant I might have a right to feel offended for him encroaching on my slot. But I didn't. Of course it was a heavy fish, and I picked up and got out of the way and settled back to watch the fun. For a long time, Mc was really serious. I don' t think it had anything to do with his upcoming marriage—or whatever he had been doing with his buddies back in the cabin. At one point, the fish was so far out in the lake that Mc's line looked as if it were a kite string bellied by the wind. I came over and called the action like a boxing announcer, an attempt at a certain levity to keep the moment in perspective. Finally, Mc reached back and handed me the new net he had bought for just this occasion. I raised my eyebrows like *you sure?* Mc shrugged his shoulders: *What do we got to lose?* I waded out with the net and used it.

I suppose my big fear is ending up like my grandfather. I don't mean that to belittle him in any way. It's the circumstances of it all that frighten me. I don't want to be another spirited, honest, hardworking sportsman fishing out his dying days for sorrowful, ill-bred trout. I know nobody can make me do it. But the thing is, I know I'm probably going to keep fishing, and in a certain light, I can worry about what it is there'll be left to fish for then. And why.

One of the last times I saw my grandfather, he was in Saint Jude's Hospital in Long Beach following a cataract operation. I was coming off the road, as I often was back then, and I brought him a quart of Schlitz to try and cheer him up. He wouldn't touch it. I drew the bottle out of the brown paper sack, holding it so Grandpa could see it with the one eye that wasn't patched. He shook his head no, saying he'd love to but he couldn't.

"The Sisters can smell it," he said.

I think about that nearly every time I fish anymore. I don't want to be seventy-five years old and afraid of anybody—certainly not anyone who stands alongside God. I don't expect to get anything out of fishing other than this: a certain peace of mind because I've stepped with respect and maybe even some decency through the ellipses between wild fish, instead of coercing gross replicas to inhabit wastelands of my own making. I guess I just think it's awfully damn important we remember, to paraphrase Thoreau, that "trout are more beautiful than they are useful."

My fish came up after the tiny emerger, rushing it at the surface, and then, after missing, pouncing twice across the chop until it connected. The phrase "Greedy take" crossed my mind, followed by the words "gluttonous," "voracious" and, yes, "piggish"—and then an image of my retriever Lucy, the way she hits the water in pursuit of *anything*.

"Guess he wanted it," said Mc, reeling up to clear the way.

We were into darkness by the time I finished. The only bad part was when the fish rushed the inlet. After I backed up and regained some order, my line was caught beneath a sliver of wood on the footbridge. I just walked over, stooped down, and freed it. I think the fish was still panting from its long run. Mc got the trout in the net and released, and we did our high fives, both of us laughing about the spirited take.

"Doesn't get any better!" Mc said, carried away by the moment, our fish, and perhaps his own foreseeable future. "Sure glad you got that pig off the bridge."

"So am I. Had I lost it, I might have cried."

Sucker
FROM SEPIC'S JOURNALS

I know what you're thinking."

The words, my own, cause the light to shift in my father's eyes. My father looks over at me, his eyes revealed by glare of the Coleman lantern. Potatoes, onions, and garlic fill the plate in front of him, the ratio dramatically disproportionate from the typical favoritism paid the mundane spud. There's a big dollop of salsa already bleeding into an edge of the mix, and a breath of heat rises from flour tortillas nestled in a blue-and-white-checked dishcloth. The beans in a skillet in the middle of the table—encircled as if by points of the compass by four long-necked beer bottles, two empty, two full—are just too gnarly for words.

"You're thinking 'How does he do it?'" I continue. I spoon a mound of refried beans on top of the food already on the plates. "That's what you're thinking. Yes? With a few simple ingredients, nothing more than a Coleman stove and the crudest of utensils, he manages time and again to come up with a veritable gastronomic masterpiece. How *does* he do it!"

My father nods, his lips wrinkled. His eyes shift between the food and me, a squint to them as he recognizes the full import of what's been placed before him. I recall this gaze throughout my life, most memorably the first time, in grade school, when I proudly presented my certain-to-be-award-winning health-science essay, "Don't Shit in Public Places."

"You know, you're right." He takes a long swig from the second beer, steeling himself for the meal. He waits for grace, which I perform with a random wave of my hand. Then he loads a tortilla, ignoring what's going inside. "That's exactly what I'm thinking: 'How *does he* do it?'"

Lucy sticks her nose up on the table. My father eyes both of us. This will be a stretch for him. I plop a big scoop of beans on top of Lucy's bowl of lamb meal and rice. She responds as if on cue, a powerful display that suggests she, at least, had enjoyed her lunch of similar rations. My father takes another long hit of beer, sighting down the length of it, closer than I thought to finishing his second bottle.

Yes, it was a tough night for my father. He had just flown in that morning, and rather than inconvenience Kay with a houseguest on top of the day-care kids, we set off directly for the North Fork. We hadn't had time, however, to see the best water. My father's knees being what they are, we settled at dusk in the Forest Service campground. On a weekday early in the season, nobody else was around. Problems with Lucy would only be our own.

But until my father got a good look at, and chance to fish, my favorite stretch of river, he was helpless, having to suffer yet another night listening to his only son's pellucid divinations, unbridled optimism, heartfelt presentiments, and overall nauseating lack of objectivity. Not to mention a woefully obstinate dog with bad gas.

The toughest part, however, would be the inevitable subject of my future. It always was. At every age—sixteen, twenty-one, thirty-two—I stood, in my father's words, "at the precipice of life." How he loved that word: *precipice*. For me, it never fails to conjure up an image of Wile E. Coyote two steps *beyond* the edge, his attention riveted on the elusive Roadrunner until, suddenly, he discovers he's in midair, about to plummet. Slowly, I've come to accept that as long as I dwelled in the future, I was attempting to capture the uncatchable, with no place to go but down. The only thing certain about the future is that it will turn out differently than I imagined. I was banking on trust, a faith in what is as what is right, the peace and freedom possible only through the wisdom of ignorance of what lies up around the bend.

"Wisdom of *ignorance?*"

My father about roars. He covers his face with his hands. We are in front of the campfire now, the wet spring cedar smoldering vainly in the undersized Forest Service pit. Lucy lies between us, emitting smells like neglected death. Our beer bottles cast faint, dancing shadows across the camp-loop drive.

"Well, I mean, we're ignorant of everything other than that it's all going to work out." My father sighs, a newfound patience of later years.

"So let's say I decide to punch you in the nose," he offers.

"There's a direction to things," I declare. "And that direction is good."

"Shit flows downhill."

"Words of wisdom," I agree.

We sat in silence, the sound of the river in high water filling the still, forested night. After a week of snow and subfreezing days, temperatures suddenly had climbed into the sixties. For two days, wind from the south felt straight out of a dryer vent. You could see trouble coming. You could *feel* it coming. Warm rains fell, and the entire Willamette watershed had backed up, unable to funnel into the Columbia, the Columbia into the sea. Yet we were high enough upriver that the flooding already had abated. What was to come downstream, the danger and destruction, had passed. My father and I sat in the silence of our own departed perils, our own immutable directions, one as unfathomable to the other as rocks in a stream. And as perfectly aligned. This was as close to arguing as we ever got, a delicate balance between reason, opinion, and faith. Mostly, we hated to ruin our time together. The obstacles that such stratagems posed to real intimacy, we had decided long ago, were more than made up for by what it meant as father and son to still be going on fishing trips together this far into our own, separate lives.

"So what *are* you going to do?"

My father reached down and scratched Lucy behind the ear. She rolled obediently onto her back, exposing herself to come what may. Delinquent as ever, I explained my intention to play things by ear.

My father gave me his all-time number-one goddamn-son-you're-hopeless look, the same one he reserved for my theories of parenting, solutions to environmental issues, instructions on how to execute a particularly difficult cast, or, more recently, schemes for dog training without inflicting pain. It was an expression somewhere between what one might expect from someone eating a sour grape and what you look like when you hit your thumb with a hammer. Yet our entire relationship was based simply on being available when one or the other asked for help. Or to go fishing. Neither of us had the heart to jeopardize that now.

"So let me show you my new rod."

It was that or defend myself. I went to the van and pulled out my latest creation. God, I can be proud of these things. I held the butt into the Coleman glare, showing off the diamond wrap, the glass-smooth finish. This one was right up there with my best. I'd named it Sin.

"*Sin?*" asked my father.

"Yeah. As in, 'Pretty as . . .'"

"But it isn't. It's ugly."

"*Ugly?*"

"Well . . . *tasteless.*"

Now, who says all of the wraps need to be the same color? Who says you can't change colors between one foot of the guide and the other? Who says you can't use every color of the rainbow in the diamond wrap *and* the guides, producing the effect of a period piece anchored brilliantly to this remarkable epoch between a nation's first acid trip and the rebirth of religious rationalization in the guise of spirituality upon the coming of the millennial New Age? I mean, hey—you think the fish notice?

"I think it's cool," I contended mildly.

My father gave up. He announced he was hitting the sack. We settled down inside my big cabin tent. Lucy launched herself off the walls as if from vertically arranged trampolines until I was able to nab her and pin her down alongside my sleeping bag. The boys shifted, reconfiguring like spoons one inside another. We could hear the river.

"We going to catch any fish tomorrow?"

But in the morning, we discovered the Glory Hole was gone. That is to say, the pool was still there, and there was still water in it, but the river had departed, changed course, undermined a two-hundred-foot fir that toppled to its death, its enormous root ball damming the head of the pool while opening a new path, a new throat, through which the entire North Fork turned and spilled, plunging its way round what was now an island and might one day—when the Glory Hole eventually dried up for good—become but the far bank, a moist hollow of ferns beyond.

The river had torn away half of the Cathedral Camp. Two of the old cedars appeared destined to fall. We recognize this sort of cataclysmic dynamism as the true beauty of old-growth forests, untamed rivers, and wilderness beaches, the very tension within our souls. But it hurts sometimes to see it all played out.

We stood on the flat tangent of the massive trunk of the fallen fir, the river rushing beneath us at the top of its new course. The Glory Hole lay still, quiet, motionless. Its dark surface reflected the high, steep bank above, just beginning to bathe in the soft greens of early spring. Patch and Speed clung tightly to our hands, both of them thrilled by the noisy power of the river racing directly below. Lucy sat staring down into the water, mesmerized by the motion. My new rod Sin felt like a weapon in my hand.

Then I saw a rise. It wasn't a big fish—they never were in the Glory Hole—and it rose near what used to be the tailout, where the smallest trout in the pool would reside. Lucy saw it, too. Somehow, she had tuned in to either the sight or sound—or both—of fish feeding on the surface, perhaps sensitive to nothing more than my own intensity and focus at such moments. I tried to stop her, snubbing up on the leash until she was off the tree, jerked midflight in the opposite direction. But unless I could hold seventy pounds of water-crazed dog dangling above the river, I was going swimming, too.

I let go. At the same moment she hit the water, so did Patch. My father kept hold of Speed and grabbed my arm, and we all teetered back into balance. Before I could jump, Patch had his arms around Lucy's neck, riding her howling down the heart of the bastard pool. We scrambled off the tree. When the pair of them reached slack water, I was out waist-deep in my chest waders, scooping Patch out of the cold, high flow.

"Patch, you were swimming!" —holding him tight to my pounding chest.

"Swimming? I was *drowning!*" —his arms around my neck, legs pressed to my sides, his strong little body shivering against mine.

I hurried back with him to the van, toweled him off, and got him into dry clothes. I don't think he was sure what had just happened. I don't know that I knew, either. Surely, he was never in any real danger. I would have been in there with him if he hadn't had Lucy to grab. We'd be telling this one the rest of our lives: "Remember when you fell in the stream and held onto Lucy and I picked you up and you said . . ."

I combed his hair, something I rarely did for either boy. Lucy bounded about in the van, oblivious to anything beyond the end of her nose. I remember hoping suddenly my father had found some water to fish with Speed. We were parked at the end of a narrow logging spur, alongside a clear-cut, and I could see where the high water had opened up the earth, first hauling off every trace of organic matter, then getting into the soil and sand and stone, carving a gash that might one day stabilize, settle into itself, to serve as seedbed for the offspring of dying grass and flowers blown heavenward on the wind. Below the fresh scar hung a deep pool that would have to hold one good fish, the dark water pressed up to a tangle of logs and limbs and branches, almost like a beaver dam, the wood still covered with bark, pine needles still clinging here and there, nothing yet stripped bare and naked, bleached by the brief summer sun.

And you would never catch that fish, I thought, speaking to myself, *never ever ever ever,* the fly impossible to swing beneath the jam, and even if the fish moved, it would spit the fly before you felt it, and even if you hooked it, it would bury you somewhere in the depths of the hole, in some dark corner of safety it had been blessed with by the raging flood.

There had to be a moment when Patch was raped, I thought suddenly, when his assailant knew what he was doing and it was all bad and he decided to do it anyway. Is this the moment out of which our lives begin?

I pulled a wool cap over Patch's damp hair and hollered for Lucy. We found my father and Speed casting in the severed Glory Hole. There was a decent hatch coming off, little flurries of the big March Browns, and fish were feeding on the surface, the rings left by some of the rises revealing trout the size you can't ignore. But I didn't like it. The way I saw it, my father and Speed were fishing in a grave, a dead part of the river, a pool left by a stream that had turned away. I let Lucy race ahead into the water, her mouth gulping gleefully, her front paws splashing. She passed directly through my father's casting lane. He threw up his arms and shouted. I told him we shouldn't be fishing there.

"Why the hell not?" he asked, surprised. There were plenty of fish there, and if they were going to die anyway, it didn't matter if we caught them first. I said he was right, it didn't matter, but I didn't know why, we weren't going to fish there.

I put Patch down, and he ran over to his brother. Speed had backed out of the water, balancing the big fly rod vertically in his hands. I looked at my father and tried to see him differently. He was exactly like I was. My two sons stood close together, watching us, the strange moment stirring their fears. I was certain nothing else was going to happen. We weren't going to fish there, and that was that.

My father turned away and cast. I walked out into the water and grabbed his line. I slid my hand down and broke off the fly at the tippet. I said "Please Dad, let's go." I was crying now, and I gathered Speed and Patch close to me and called to Lucy and headed for the van. It didn't matter if he followed. It didn't matter if he stayed and fished. It was his choice, and I was making my own.

We spent the next two days fishing a long, ugly reservoir behind a dam that had flooded a forgotten stretch of a fork of the big river that would have had to have been, in its time, as good as any. The entire drainage was still overflowing. The closest thing to fishable river we'd found had been right there in the reaches above and below the Glory Hole. But even that water had been too heavy, too much for young boys or an elderly fisherman without good knees or practice, lately, fishing a steep, wooded stream or wading deep.

We fished from a high-sided rented aluminum boat, propelled by a five-horsepower outboard that started each time on the very first pull. This delighted my father, who manned the motor from his driver's position at rear of the craft. The boys and I sat forward, facing him. Lucy stayed near the bow, though at times when anchored or drift fishing we had to tie her there to keep her from swimming. We caught fish off and on throughout both days, rainbows of eight to ten inches, usually on bait, worms or salmon eggs, although a couple times my father picked up fish casting and retrieving a little Super Duper. We also spent hours trolling, the boys and Lucy sleeping close to me, tucking their heads inside their coats to escape the wind, drifting off to the drone of the motor.

Some of the fish we kept and killed. Some we released, and I would like to say, bait fishing what it is, they probably died anyway. But I don't know that for sure. I was glad the boys had so many opportunities to actually witness fish dying, because I'd rarely provided them that priceless lesson, the only one coming to mind being the first and only trout I killed with Patch on the North Fork. Maybe there were others in Baja with Speed when he was very young. I'm not exactly sure. But it goes a long, long way in our understanding of things to experience the life and fight of an animal—even a domestic trout with every ounce of true spirit lost to interbreeding—and then see that creature dead, inert, visually identical, yet dissimilar in every aspect, the difference the dismissal of its soul. I don't know what had gotten into me.

The last afternoon we went after The Big One. It had become a joke between my father and me since the time Peter and I convinced him, in all earnestness and the wake of some tequila, to rig up one evening at Punta Chivato on the Sea of Cortez with fifty-pound test and cast out an ungodly wad of bait alongside a tuft of rocks. My father took it pretty seriously. Only later, while standing all alone in the new-moon darkness, did he realize he didn't really wish to fish like that, Big One or not. No doubt, like most anglers, he had learned that same lesson before, but in all the professed excitement—Peter and I being how we are sometimes—my father simply forgot. Me, I've caught plenty of Big Ones—as has my father—but I've never caught one while trying for it, other than that's what I'm always trying to catch, if that makes any sense.

Still, it was part of my father's notion of a fishing trip. Unlike me, he felt any fishing preferable to putting the rods down, so if nothing else was happening, he might as well try for The Big One. What that meant was bait—a lot of it—on a tight line above a sinker on the bottom, and then waiting—a lot of that, too. Basically, it was how I'd first been taught to fish. It was crude, mindless, and terribly effective. I believed in it the way I believed in evil. I understood its power, its seductive nature, and I had avoided it since puberty the same way I avoided women with more emotional problems than I had: usually, but not always.

The first bump came, as they will, while everybody was paying attention to something else. Or to nothing. We were fishing close to the dam in the perceived deepest part of the reservoir, our rods limp over the sides, sodas open all around. Then my father said "Whoa." It wasn't an exclamation, merely an observation. He pointed to Speed's rod, and Speed perked up. There was another little bump, and then a series in quick succession, and then Speed was tight to the fish and reeling, losing line all the while.

Now, part of the method when soaking bait was that we always kept our drags backed way off, especially on the youngsters' reels. Speed had a cheap little Abu Garcia I had bought for him to use until he became effective enough with a fly rod to give up completely on spinning gear, then pass it down to Patch, and while my father hollered at him to keep his tip up, I reached over and tightened the drag a bit. But the line continued to pour out. This is when I hate spinning reels most. They're easy to cast, a child in kindergarten can fish one alone, and the small, pricey models are elegant little machines on the order of spring-wound watches or the classic Volkswagen 1600 engine. But by its very nature, a spinning reel can't fight a good fish the way a good fish needs to be fought.

It wasn't long before Speed got tired of reeling. He wasn't getting anywhere, anyway. I had to convince my father to let Patch have a turn, my father being of the strong opinion that he or I should take over. I asked him what he thought it might be, food for winter? I shouldn't have said that. My father let me know it by pouting until Patch, too, was worn out by the fish. Then I offered the rod to my father.

"No, you go ahead," he said, as casually as a heavyweight in a clinch. I just handed him the rod and said let's see what it is.

My father fiddled with the drag, tried to gauge the weight of the fish a time or two, and then looked over at me and nodded— an expression that meant "It's for real." Then he went to work on the fish. He started lifting and reeling, lifting and reeling, the famed pumping action of big-game fishing and beer commercials that nobody pays attention to after the fish first jumps, or runs off line a dozen or so times. I mean, it was just a damn lake, not like the ocean, where you can, theoretically, catch *anything*.

Still, I admit my interest had become more than passing. So was Lucy's. She hung her nose over the side, peering down into the black water, her tail beating against the aluminum in time to the spin of the handle in my father's hand. When the fish bore down and peeled off a new chunk of line, her tail rapped briefly in double time. Then the fish was there next to the boat, for all of us to see.

"My God, it's a *sucker*!"

"What's that?" asked my father.

"Take a look," I said.

True faith is knowing that all things are of God, I thought, *and God is good*. Speed and Patch watched the big fish rolling side to side like an Iowa hog wallowing in the mud. Speed observed it was gross. These vague generalizations are the stuff of future stereotyping. I pointed out that the fish's scales were, well, *remarkable* scales.

"And look at that mouth," I added, warming to the beast. "Perfectly adapted for the ecological niche that the species has blessed us by filling!"

"We don't have a net," countered my father.

As if on cue once more, Lucy went into the water. She struggled with the fish, growing more excited by the moment as my father shouted he'd kill her. Then she lifted the fish in her mouth from the lake—at least the middle of it. The head and tail still draped onto the surface. It was almost too good to be true. It *was* too good to be true. The fish secure in her mouth, Lucy took off swimming for the distant shore.

"I'll *kill* that dog!" repeated my father.

"Over my dead body," I stated—precisely as such occasions demand.

Lucy didn't look back. All two hundred years of breeding had kicked in like wild horses, and the generation or two she seemed to have missed out on were certainly not going to slow her down. Nor was my father with the little spinning reel. We shipped anchor and began to get dragged across the lake, my father cinching down on the drag as tight as he dared.

It wasn't nearly enough. By my calculations, the reel would be empty long before we reached shore. My father did everything he could to make Lucy fight against the rod, trying to wear her out, but she paddled merrily along, her head held high in the manner of her New England ancestors watching out for ice floes. She really is quite the dog.

"If we lose this fish . . ."

"If we lose it, *what?*" I asked, enjoying Lucy's performance. "I mean, who gives a f—."

I raised my hand to my mouth, remembering my sons.

"I mean, *who cares?* You saw what that thing looks like. You can't tell me landing it *matters*."

"It's the principle of the thing." My father turned away, gazing out at the dog and fish at the distant end of his line. "Can't you at least understand that?"

Well, I could. I really could. I could understand that. I suppose that's why I was his son, he was my father.

I put up my fly rod. I'd brought it along in the boat, my own "principle of the thing." I tied on the biggest streamer I had with me, not nearly as big as I wanted, but it would have to do. I directed the boys and my father to shift around, clear the decks so to speak, and then I peeled off line, letting it fall in a loose pile on top of the cooler. My first cast wasn't in the ballpark. But after that, I started to get some real distance, double-hauling for the life of me.

"*LUCY!*" I finally shouted.

She turned her head and spotted the streamer fluttering down to the water. Without blinking, she was after it. I can still picture the sight clearly, my profound, brown dog with the soft, floppy ears bearing down on the fly with an enormous sucker held crossways in her mouth. Speed and Patch cheered. My father silently reeled in slack line. I just kept retrieving, pausing each time Lucy momentarily lost sight of the fly, ripping it back at me to catch her attention again.

This time, we didn't need a net. Lucy swam right to the boat. There was a last, furious surge of excitement while she clamored up over the side, throwing paws and water in all directions. By the time I got her halfway settled, my father held the fish, a nasty gash showing through its protective armor of scales.

"Oh, look!" I said, pointing. "She bit the Big One!"

"Do I let it go?"

My father held the sucker over the side. Lucy pressed forward, trying to get at the fish. I held her collar, her eyes darting back and forth between my father and me.

"I think they're considered hard on the planted crop," I said. I reached out and took the fish with my free hand, running my fingers through one set of gills, my thumb through the other. Then I punched the sucker's head one time hard against the edge of the aluminum boat.

"Pop!" exclaimed Patch and Speed, the gleeful terror of youth in their voices.

"But I imagine they make terrific dog food," I added, laying the fish at Lucy's feet.

My father sat shaking his head.

"Some 'purist,'" he said.

"Some fish," I offered, drawing my two sons to my side.

The World's Sexiest Fly-Fishing Show
FROM SEPIC'S JOURNALS

*T*his requires I go back a ways.

Her name was Lythandra Prewd, the counselor Kay and I were seeing when I finally decided to get Lucy. *His* name was Philip Brieseldorf, a friend of Ms. Prewd's whom she suggested I get ahold of when I let on about my history as a fly fisherman in the surf.

It could get complicated if I let it. But the outcome was, I met Breiseldorf in the gardens at Bishop's Close one day shortly after the floods, and he asked if I would do a show for a fishing club, the Rose City Fly Rodders, of which he was the president. Though flattered, I was ambivalent about the proposal until we descended the path to the cliffs overlooking Elk Rock Island, where Breiseldorf placed his palms to his chest, gazed out over the cocoa-colored river, and recited a poem:

O, like the stormy surf in my breast
Run the wild rivers of passion
Hell-bent full of love
Tumbling without thought
To the waiting placid arms of Oceans
Spread mightily to all far corners of glorious Earth
Pressed limitlessly complete of Life
Great salmon and trout one Spirit—

at which point I asked, "Hey, weren't you on the McCloud around, say, 1980?"

Breiseldorf squatted, tipped forward onto his hands, and shot out his legs. He raised up onto his fingertips, then balanced on both thumbs and performed a series of rapid pushups.

"I thought you'd never notice," he said, bouncing to his feet.

"Do you have my leather jacket?" I asked.

Time had not been kind to Breiseldorf. He was stout as a boot, bald as a heel. He wore a goatee as creepy as the hair between the pads of Lucy's paws. He had a gold ring on his thumb. But I could see he had made some peace with the world, if only as tenuous as my own. Sensing fate in all of this, I agreed to try my hand at a show if he would let me experiment with something other than the usual go-here, do-this, catch-these kind of rigmarole. He thought about it a moment, then nodded his wrinkled head, suggesting I solicit the help of Lythandra Prewd, our mutual acquaintance.

"Why Prewd?" I asked, sensing myself in a current deeper than I imagined.

"No real reason," said Breiseldorf. He licked his fingertips and began polishing his skull. "Other than that she's been talking about this ever since you mentioned how heroic it feels wading out into surf with nothing but a fly rod, a pair of Speed-os, and a head-dress full of bold, brilliant flies."

Heroic?

"It's a moral outrage!"

Kay flung my poster advertising The World's Sexiest Fly-Fishing Show onto the dining room table. She had tried to convince me to revise my efforts, appealing to reasons of taste, industry goodwill, and the affect on our family name. Now was the time for the descent into dramatics, the level of most of our discussions of late.

"You've gone too far," she said, placing her fingertips to her temples and twisting her head side to side.

I reinspected my handiwork. The part I liked best—besides the title—was the tall, narrow picture of Lythandra Prewd herself, decked out in fishing vest, hip waders, flesh-colored panties, and not a stitch else. She stood with her backside toward the camera, bent slightly at the waist, her hands stroking the feathers of a big, white streamer locked in the jaws of a tying vise, her face peering over her shoulder, eyes staring directly at the viewer. I had placed the italicized subtitle—*In The Surf*—such that it was difficult to tell, unless you looked really close, whether there was actually anything covering her derriere at all.

"Well, I agree it's a little out there," I said. "But—"

"A little '*out there!?*' It's a goddamn moral—"

"Got it."

I raised my hands in surrender. The rest of the poster included a pair of shots of big, empty surf, immaculate wind-sculpted barrels as finely shaped as conch shells. Around these, an array of fish, both dead and alive, cradled lovingly by yours truly, courtesy of my pal Peter. Except for the pose of Prewd, it was all pretty tame—just your typical invitation to an orgy of tight lines, bent rods, and expensive, screaming reels.

"It lacks *subtlety*," announced Kay, refusing to let it lie.

By the time I arrived home from the latest trip to the North Fork, Breiseldorf had left a string of phone messages announcing updates on ticket sales and changing venue locations. One place after another had become too small. The Bridgetown Brewery, site of most the R.C. Fly Rodders' monthly meetings, held fifty, tops, and the Raw Deal, reserved for industry elites, was only twice as big. Frantic, Breiseldorf left a message in the middle of the week saying he had weighed all options and chosen to rent a midsized conference room at the Red Lion in Jantzen Beach. Then came a series of brief, unintelligible reports that pleaded for my immediate return and/or demise, the garble as a whole spanning approximately forty-eight hours. Finally, in a voice as serene as Jell-O, Breiseldorf proclaimed he had procured the perfect place, once and for all, that in fact he felt *led* to this spot, that each step closer had appeared as if by miracle, actually guiding him from one choice through the next. The World's Sexiest Fly-Fishing Show would be held in the sanctuary of The Church of One—seating capacity 1,000.

"'Kind of church is that, Phil?"

I held the phone tucked between my ear and shoulder, sorting through an impressive stack of junk mail and bills.

"It's called a New Thought church," answered Breiseldorf. "They believe we're all one. They believe we're all God."

"Imagine that," I said, tossing all of the mail but my disability check into the recycling bin. "Doesn't sound that new to me, though."

"Don't tell me you know this stuff?"

"I wouldn't, Phil. What you don't know can't hurt you."

"That scares me. That really does." I heard Breiseldorf take a slow deep breath on the other end of the line. "In fact, ever since you had that poster printed I've been feeling a little, well—"

"Fear is your ego speaking."

"God help me, pal!"

"He will, Phil. He will."

It turned out our friend Lythandra Prewd had been the one to put Breiseldorf in contact with the church. Still cradling the phone, I dug my vise out of my travel kit and clamped it to the bench, and while Breiseldorf explained his path to the church sanctuary, I went to work on my new Big Surf Series, inspired by the flood damage we'd seen in the North Fork watershed. Mostly, I intended to tie up some enormous rainbow-spectrum streamers along the lines of the new rod Sin, confident I could get anglers in Oregon to bite, so to speak, on just about anything. Not that I wanted to mislead anybody. My first and fundamental belief in surf fishing with flies is that anything could work. And most things do, if fished right and with enough faith.

It also appeared that Kay's critique of my poster was prophetic. The level of interest was such that the last thing this show was going to be about was subtleties.

"They did ask we promise one thing," confided Breiseldorf. I layered in a pair of teal-blue saddle hackles, an effect as abrupt as van Gogh's use of pure red lines in facial skin. I leaned over and winked at Lucy.

"What's that, Phil?"

"That the talk not be . . . well . . . you know . . . profane."

"*Profane?*"

"Yeah. Like your poster."

I tied in two pairs of grizzly saddle hackle dyed yellow, the fly already pushing the size of a small mullet.

"Phil, what's going on? You don't sound so jolly anymore."

"These religious sorts make me nervous. You don't know what they're really thinking."

"Sure you do, Phil. It's just like you said: 'We're all one. We're all God.'"

"*That's* what makes me nervous," declared Breiseldorf. "That sort of talk sounds subversive!"

Now for *la gran puta*: I built in one, two, three wads of jet-black bucktail, which exploded from the madly colored background like Lucy in the midst of a toddlers' Easter-egg hunt.

"Phil, did you make that promise? Did you make that promise, Phil?"

"I had to. It was either that or keep searching. And I felt *led* to the place."

"By . . . *what?*" I don't know why *that* thought occurred to me. "What is this all about, Phil?"

"Well, I mean—"

"No, don't tell me. Don't tell me, Phil You'll start making *me* nervous."

I opened the vise jaws and let the big fly fall free. In my hand, it looked even worse, one of those remarkably ugly flies you tie now and then, so bad you're embarrassed to let it enter a box or fly wallet for fear it will pollute the others. Or that somebody you know might see it. All of a sudden, I felt rusty.

"Phil, I'm absolutely sure you've been led to wherever we're doing this show. That's why I'm going to keep that promise of yours. I really am."

"You promise?"

"I promise."

I don't think I was the cause of it all. I really don't. Not all of it.

The church was located in the abandoned state mental hospital in a suburb south of Portland that is beginning to look a lot like Orange County—after the oranges. The sanctuary itself felt like it might have once served as a cafeteria, a bowling alley, a bathhouse. I mean, you couldn't tell what it had been. Maybe a video arcade. I have an aunt who would know, but since it was always assumed she worked there for fear of ending up inside as a patient instead, I wouldn't feel right asking.

The church had tried to mask the institutional flavor of the room with sedate, pastel-colored paint and low-voltage fluorescent lights, that queer juxtaposition of means favored by corporations, motor vehicle departments, power companies, and a certain type of man or woman in need or on the make. Does that include everybody? The embracing nature of the sanctuary was diminished, however, by the vast number of enlargements reproduced from my original poster, many of them cropped to contain only the Lythandra Prewd panel, blown up life-size to reveal every nuance of her imposing, insensitive gaze.

"I thought we were concerned about *profanity*," I remarked, standing offstage with Breiseldorf while the house began to fill.

"We were." Breiseldorf caught Ms. Prewd's eye. He waved to her onstage as she performed a series of abrupt guttural noises for the sound guys in the balcony. "But Lythandra insisted."

I first noticed my sense of discomfort, all things considered, when Breiseldorf again waved to Ms. Prewd, one of those cootchy-cootchy, all-fingers-moving-separately-at-once waves that Grandma will perform for anybody's infant in a stroller. And why in God's name was this woman wearing *waders* beneath her full-length, embroidered Smith & Hawken Oaxacan skirt?

"She's both a church member *and* the newest member of the Rose City Fly Rodders," observed Breiseldorf, as if reading my mind. "We should feel fortunate for her accepting the role of liaison."

"You sure we don't have a conflict of interests?"

"She's in charge," announced Breiseldorf. "She's in *charge*."

Ms. Prewd nodded toward the balcony, motioning someone there to lower the projection screen behind her. The screen settled into place, nearly as wide as the stage, where Christ might hang in a different church, with just enough room to one side for a pair of mauve leather chairs. She signaled again, and the big screen filled with a photo I remembered all too well, a close-up of a big red snapper held in such a way as to reveal the imprint of a box of Camels seen through my soaked trunks. In fact, you could see more than that. And this with the lights still on.

"Jesus Christ, Phil! That woman has balls!"

Breiseldorf looked directly at me. The glare from the projector seemed to press his eyes back into his shiny bald head. For a moment he looked as if he were attempting to dislodge a wad of phlegm from his throat, his big goatee twitching like a suffocating rodent. Then the projector shut off, the screen rose slowly, and with that sinking feeling I associate with a tight line gone slack, I watched as Ms. Prewd performed that classic pumping gesture we all remember from childhood when attempting to inspire the drivers of semi trucks to blast their horns. Ms. Prewd, however, employed both fists, not one, her face a joyful grimace.

My concern rose as the folding chairs filled and the crowd began lining the walls—both sides and in back. Kay and the boys, my father, Mc, and his new wife all sat in a special section reserved to one side of the stage. The room grew not only crowded, but uncomfortably warm. I liked the effect this would have with the Baja slides, but I had begun to imagine that this might not really be about fishing at all. The worst thing is not knowing. *Who's running this show, anyway?*

But it still seemed okay when Breiseldorf stepped to the pulpit and opened the meeting. You could tell he was well liked by the regulars, and his easy manner and goofy good looks disarmed the visitors, even the hard-core guys along the peripheries whose cool, expressionless stares said "This better be good." He was especially helped by Miss Prewd, whom Breiseldorf thanked effusively for her efforts to secure the sanctuary, to which she responded by turning her back to the crowd and lifting her Mexican skirt high above the tops of hip waders, while reenacting perfectly the impressive gaze from our poster and her own life-sized blowups. The only difference was that now she was clearly covered by nothing more than the thin black line of a G-thong affixed to a wading belt, with the phrase "SURF'S UP!" planted smartly across her pale, narrow tush, one word per cheek.

I watched Kay and my father, who had never been particularly close, exchange looks in three shades of red. They gathered up the boys and headed for the exit. Mc gave his new wife a sharp glance, however, that said *You stay right where you are!* And I have to admit, Ms. Prewd showed a real flare for this kind of thing, the sort of talent adults across the board can appreciate, so that I don't think anybody but my own family felt truly *compelled* to get the hell out of Dodge.

Still, this was the moment my fear really began to take hold. These people had come looking for something, and suddenly I suffered serious doubts that I was going to be able to deliver—at least not the goods they were after. The sensation was much like hooking an especially good fish, the grim mix of glee and panic that basically boils down to railing at yourself not to screw this thing up. Yet while I had settled of late on the belief that landing or losing a fish didn't ever really matter, not in the grand scheme of things, it jumped out at me all at once that the crowd out there might be direfully more attached to the outcome of things. And it wouldn't be about the ten bucks. It never was. Without a wisp of exaggeration, it could be proven with hard numbers that the average cost of every pound of fish caught by the fly rodders in front of me was in the neighborhood of two, three, four, maybe five hundred dollars. And almost any one of them wouldn't hesitate to drop another hundred, easy, if I could provide a single tip that would guarantee that he or she would catch something, anything, *double the local average.* Yet here I was preparing to stand up and tell them—with pictures!—of blazing, red-hot fishing available to each and every one of them simply by loading up a car and heading south, then turning either left or right, and stopping at the beach where land ends. That's it. *Finito. Nada mas.* Cast from the edge.

What was I thinking? They'd never buy it.

The next time Ms. Prewd came onstage, she was accompanied by music, a woeful sax solo that brought to mind every time you've looked at the sea and descended into cheap, sentimental blues. She was also without the skirt altogether, the major portion of her crucial aspects hidden by the poster fishing vest, to which she'd attached a dense array of brightly-dyed hackle necks and bucktails as a sort of peekaboo fringe dangling to the tops of her waders.

I was glad for the break. I had been laboring through the technical portion of my talk—lines, rods, reels—the part I liked least because there wasn't much to it, once you got beyond the basics. I sensed the crowd growing restless. From the start, I had mixed in a high percentage of fish slides to go along with the less exciting shots of gear and spectacular scenery, but Ms. Prewd's leering presence established a tone I was having trouble matching. Granted, I had saved the best shots for later—the bent rods and arched backs, the gloriously brilliant big fish still alive, dripping with surf—but my gut feeling was Ms. Prewd was carrying the show. Not that I resented it. We had clearly outstripped our wildest expectations of the gross. Now I was simply afraid we couldn't finish what we had started.

The chanting began while I was making my appeal for catch-and-release ethics in any and all manner of fishing. I do believe fly fishing is part of the natural evolution of every angling career, but merely fishing with flies and fly rods is nobody's salvation. A lot of people don't like to hear that. A lot of people think that if they fish with flies, they're hot stuff. A lot of us have thought ourselves more than that. When the truth is, the only fishing that can save any of us is the kind that doesn't hurt a single soul—including our own.

"Prewd! Prewd! Prewd! Prewd!"

She came out once in a cellophane wet suit. Or maybe it was see-through Lycra. I don't keep up with this stuff the way I used to. I had included a number of surf shots—short boards, long boards, nose rides, tube rides—to try to give the full dimension of what the sport I was talking about implied. A guy paddles out, catches a wave, and dances to the tune of symphonic forces inspired by the heart of the spirit in all things. Like each fish, every wave is plugged in to the divine. Yet it is only at the edge of the ocean, beyond the sure and steady land, that we are able to stand and feel the surf and the grace from which it comes. Both fish and waves travel countless miles through the sea, essentially meaningless until they brush up against shore. Only there, only then, when the wave breaks, the fish strikes the fly, are we able to sense at some level beyond our mere intellect the immense scope of the dynamics at play. Revelation unfolds much the way that the spiraling wave traces the bend of the land, the very shape it forms and reforms, caresses, and sometimes pounds, the wave a mirror, the mirror the land. Somewhere in all of this move waves of fish, too, a surf within a surf, wild creatures propelled as schools or as one, immaculately fitted into the ebb and flow of winds and tides, the echoes of storms, the voices of stars.

Many of the surf shots I'd included were of empty, flawless waves. The brilliant Baja light and scouring winds exposed almost surreal geometry and textures, some sensual liquid anatomy nearly explosive in its radiance. Ms. Prewd positioned herself beautifully. The music was now one of those environmental mood pieces, right down to the screaming seagulls and sound of crashing surf. Her shadow grew and diminished in fitful response to the slides, the flat black silhouette impossibly dimensionless against the dazzling screen. Yet the light on her exposed body—crackling with reflections and distorted, prismatic colors—revealed all nature of the human form's strange magic, the absence of reason beyond exactly what is. She whipped that crowd into a frenzy.

I knew it was getting out of hand when one half of the house began trying to outshout the other.

"PREWD!" bellowed one side.

"*PREWD!*" echoed the other.

"PREWD!"

"*PREWD!*"

"PREWD!"

"*PREWD!*"

Then I barraged them with the best of the best. A dozen different species, nothing less than ten pounds, each fish as unique in shape and color as genera of desert wildflowers. And, naturally, the long, flexed rods, the hair-raising fights through reefs and surging shore break, the dead calm of expansive, empty beaches, the foam around headland rocks, the reach of waves to the wading angler's throat. It is altogether blasphemous, I informed my audience, that the sport of fly fishing continues to suffer emaciation due to the dietary affectations paid the solitary *Salmo/Oncorhynchus* genus. Has your ego such a stranglehold that you still think for even a moment that the marriage of fly fishing with trout, steelhead, and salmon is based on anything but illusion and sense of scarcity, a universe borne of fear, instead of love?

"Of course you don't!" I answered shouting from the pulpit. "That's why you're here!"

"PREWD! *PREWD!* PREWD! *PREWD!*"

The slide of my father came up. Thank God we were almost to the end. Ms. Prewd had brought my new rod onstage, no matter that it had never been intended for use in anything resembling surf. The balance was perfect for a woman her size. A percussion solo performed on aboriginal old-growth drift-wood filled the already overheated sanctuary, and Ms. Prewd began executing a slow-motion pantomime of each basic cast—overhand, backhand, roll, steeple, pile, single haul, double haul—her movements like T'ai Chi in their deft rhythms and elegance. My father stood there on-screen in all his glory, the enormous halibut lifeless at the end of his strong, tan arm. In his other hand the fly rod—broken, though we didn't yet know it—looks too fine and slender to have subdued the great fish, as though it were more an instrument of accompaniment than the weapon that had carried the fight. The man himself is all smiles, the blue sun and sea stacked perfectly level, one atop the other, the horizon sharp as a blade. Ms. Prewd held the rod overhead, hands apart, arms outstretched, then drew it toward her as if straining to complete one final chin-up. She rose up on her toes, furthering the illusion of ascension, the image of the big halibut passing down her upturned face, her wide-open mouth. I don't know if she knew it, but the fish looked like a monstrous green tongue.

We had done up one last slide with the rainbow streamers. It was really more of a decoration, an abstract expression of visual sensations one might experience while blind casting in the Baja surf. None of the flies actually *meant* anything. None of them had caught a fish, been cast, or even touched the sea. But to call them art would be absurd. The crowd was on its feet now, clapping, chanting, and stomping to the old Joe Cocker version of "Cry Me a River," Ms. Prewd's printed fanny pointed directly at them, rotating first in one direction of the clock, then back around in the other. During the slowdown finale, while Cocker attempts to make rock 'n' roll history by sheer force of each single cry, the lighting fell, bit by bit, until all was black except the big screen filled with the shrieking, kaleidoscopic flies. Then in a heartbeat, the room went dark, the music ended, and all at once in the spotlight stood Ms. Prewd in profile, naked as heaven on earth, an incredible appendage extending from her pelvis, my flies in real-life color aligned dramatically along the upward reach of this stunning, erect apparition—now detailed up on screen for those who couldn't believe their eyes, the sight of the living flesh.

"Are there, uh, any questions?" I asked.

The lights came on. Ms. Prewd blew the crowd a single kiss, tossing the G-thong high into the air. By the time it landed, all hell had broken loose.

Donkey's Fish
FROM SEPIC'S JOURNALS

*N*othing prepares us for the next moment. Or it all does, if we are able to see. We have reasons for everything, and then those reasons shatter. We are utterly wrong and we start all over again. We return to fly fishing because we are certain that here, at least, the good guys always win.

It was as if in that moment Lythandra Prewd changed, transformed, reverted to her former self. Or he did. Was. The truth in these matters is inscrutable. We intuit with vague clues the life beneath the surface, the mysteries within surf or stream. We haven't the foggiest. Lythandra was Lynn, and when she told me her story that night, it was something other than I ever could have imagined. Her voice became that of the person she once was, a young man whose emergence was as if aborted by the circumstances of home, family, the place in which he was raised. She had been somebody else. Yet the content remained immutable, so that even the unique, if also bizarre, story of Lythandra or Lynn Prewd was no more extraordinary than any pool's lunker, a stream changing course, a day of perfect surf "like never before." It is all to be expected, if we can but expect more than we can possibly imagine.

"Donkey said he knew where there was a big fish that year. He had seen it, he said, and he was going to catch it. Donkey was always saying things like that, like the time he found an eagle's nest in Wally's big piss fir and climbed up and stole the eggs and tried to hatch them and raise the chicks. 'The eagles are my brothers,' said Donkey, a belief too deep for any of us to deny.

"He said the big fish was in the Nigger Hole. Everyone

around Madrone called it that after an old black guy died there, or at least he was found dead, drowned, Wally said, but it was pretty hard to tell, the body had been in the river so long. People drown in the river all the time, not every year, but you know, fishermen in winter who drive in over the coast range from the valley. But a black man was like something out of the blue, an omen or a thing like that, so after that it was the Nigger Hole and still is.

"We all figured Donkey's big fish was a blessing, too—kind of like the eagle's nest, in that it would teach us something, even if we couldn't understand. Of course, we didn't know if the fish was real. Not that Donkey would lie or anything. It's just that like Wally said, everyone has seen a big fish before that doesn't exist.

"Donkey worked out a scheme where he could fish the Nigger Hole from on top of the high bank at the edge of the road. He took a stack of two-by-fours up there, or he got me and Wally to drop them off, is a better way to put it, and he nailed them together and built himself a little deck from which he could sit on his butt and cast a line down to the water. Donkey, you see, didn't have any legs. I feel weird saying that because we never thought about it anymore: Donkey was Donkey, and the reason he was called that was because he was stubborn as a god-damn mule, not because he didn't have any legs. Excuse my French, as Wally used to say.

"I guess besides Donkey having no legs, the other thing I should tell is that Wally was also kind of Donkey's stepdad. There was more to it than that. Donkey's mother, who was also my mom, disappeared from Madrone the same day Wally felled a tree in the woods across Donkey's knees. And before that, nobody but I guess maybe she knew who Donkey's real father was. Or mine, as that goes.

"For awhile it seemed like a good thing, Donkey up above the river on his little deck, fishing in the Nigger Hole for his big fish. He was there all January and on in to the next. Donkey wore a big green poncho year-round, maybe to hide the fact he didn't have legs, although that's probably not it, he looked so much like a big turtle, moving around in that thing. Anyway, it kept him half dry. For that month and then on into the next, he was there all hours of the day, the big firs and piss firs dripping on his head, the wind shaking his green poncho. When the sun came out, he steamed. He looked like a wet army sock.

"Of course, it became clear if the fish was there, Donkey was going to catch it. He had a handline made out of braided Dacron Wally gave him, and below that a big cork bobber he and I found once when we were kids, when Wally took us and Mom like he used to sometimes down to the beach by the river mouth for a picnic. Then there was some good leader, his lead slinkie, and the bait. Donkey always had pretty much whatever he needed to do whatever he wanted to do. He'd just come by and ask, and if Wally or anyone else around Madrone could help, they did.

"It was like that with the eagles. Donkey spotted the nest up in the big piss fir, the dark birds coming and going, and he climbed up arm over arm and got the eggs and came down and asked us all to help him raise them. Coming down, he looked like a green kite caught up there in the branches. A bunch of us had gathered to watch. I don't know about the others, but I was afraid for Donkey up there. I knew he was stubborn enough to do anything he put his mind to, but there was no telling what, at the moment, he had his mind on. I mean, you should have seen him. Wally's big spruce was the only one left anywhere around Madrone. All the others had been cut, but for some reason he had left one standing, a reminder of something, I guess. The ones near the river were just more or less weeds, shitty little saplings like the ones that had to be cleared if you were serious about growing real timber. They didn't even make good firewood.

"'Piss firs, piss wood,' Wally would say.

"But the real one he left standing behind his place was a tall, thick tree, big around as a big boulder at the bottom, even if it did look a little sad sometimes, standing there all alone. And when Donkey came down that day with those eagle eggs, even though I was afraid for him, I could see there were things going on in our lives bigger than any of us would ever figure out.

"We pitched in and built Donkey a little coop and a nest for the eggs. It was against the law as all get out, but around here, there's a history of doing pretty much as we please, as long as we all agree it's okay. And anything for Donkey was always the way it worked. Wally told us to build the coop right under the tree, so if the eagles returned, their shit would fall around the eggs and help them hatch. I don't know if he was kidding. Donkey sat on the eggs for weeks that spring, claiming he was their brother, not hardly moving, his stubborn face all that showed inside his poncho under Wally's tree. Stuff fell on him, but I didn't look too close to see. I just remember Donkey sitting there.

"The eggs never did hatch. Finally Donkey cracked them open and said his brothers were dead. We all felt bad. Donkey dug a deep grave by himself right there under the nest where he had been sitting beside Wally's tree, and after he buried the shells and what had been inside, he asked us to take down the coop and forgive him for doing such a stupid thing. He felt bad, too.

"'We all have the same goddamn feelings,' said Wally.

"But you had to wonder what Donkey was feeling while fishing for his big fish. You don't just sit out all January and on into the next in the cold rain and wind and not feel something. I guess he wanted that fish pretty bad. I guess he had his reasons.

"Then one day Donkey got a fish, a nice big hen pushing ten twelve pounds or so, but he said it wasn't the one. We figured he knew what he was after. The fish was a handful, even for Donkey, and he really looked like something, coming down the road that day with that dead steelhead poking out from under his poncho, like a head or a pecker, or a long slimy limb jutting out of that dripping shell. Even Wally said it was too much for words.

"Still, we were all pretty proud of Donkey. I mean, a lot of us those days didn't get a single winter fish anymore. Even those who did didn't get them right near town, not like we used to. And catching it in the Nigger Hole was a thing all of us could especially appreciate, since it had been years since anybody had even fished there, at least not any of us who lived around Madrone and knew the story.

"But Donkey told us it wasn't his fish. No one argued, because he ought to know. We went up to Wally's and had ourselves the kind of party we did sometimes, barbecued the fish and drank some beer, but before we were through, Donkey disappeared, and when we were done, we wandered up the road and found him back fishing the Nigger Hole. I told you he was stubborn. We were all kind of drunk, the way you feel half the time in the winter anyway, what with the rain and wet on you all the time and drinking beer whenever you're lucky enough to be somewhere warm and dry, so when we found Donkey, we got to kidding him and saying he was crazy.

"It's hard to tell about. There was a drizzle that night, with the lights from Wally's and the other places above Madrone sparkling in the little piss firs, so that it almost looked like stars around Donkey. I could hear the river, up above and below, the way you do sometimes even though it's always making noise, especially in winter when it's blown. Wally was over pissing his beer next to a tree, and then while we were kidding Donkey, telling him he was crazy to be out fishing when he just caught a goddamn decent fish, Wally turned and peed on the back of Donkey's poncho.

"I guess he was just drunk. Wally laughed, his dick out in the dark, and Donkey went right on fishing, like maybe he didn't notice or we weren't even there.

"I wanted to do something, but I didn't. I never know what to do when I'm afraid. Wally had been pissing long enough he hardly got any on Donkey, but that didn't mean he wasn't being mean. I still feel bad. I mean, it wasn't about whether he was crazy or not. There's nothing crazier than a legless guy in a poncho casting all January and on into the next trying to catch a big fish he says he's seen but maybe even isn't real. But that's part of a craziness in this world, not anything on your own. Donkey wasn't crazy any more than any of us. Stubborn, okay, but maybe that was his kind of courage, a way of doing things his own way. Wally said later that probably those dead eagle eggs and the old black guy was what Donkey really had on his mind down there at the end of his line that winter in the Nigger Hole. Wally always had a way of putting things.

"In the morning, Donkey was gone. I didn't know what to make of it, other than that maybe he decided the one fish was enough, after all. But that wasn't like him. I was helping Wally on a framing job up near Spruce Run that winter, inching along like all jobs in winter, and when I drove past the Nigger Hole that morning, I saw the empty deck and thought *I wonder what's up*. That evening, when I came back down, the deck was still empty. It looked lonely and even a little sad without Donkey there after all January and on into the next, but then sometimes about then each winter a lot of things seem sad if you're not careful or you haven't caught a fish.

"I asked around, and nobody had seen Donkey, either. Not even Wally. I got worried. Donkey disappeared after the eagle eggs died, but that was spring, and although it was still plenty wet, it wasn't cold the way it is in winter, and certainly not as dark. People forget about how dark it can be in winter with the rain. People forget about how low the darkness can get you feeling.

"I went looking for Donkey up and down the river. That's really the only dangerous place around. Not that I felt Donkey was in any trouble. He always knew how to take care of himself, probably better than most. But things happen, and sometimes it doesn't matter how stubborn you are, they still do.

"Up above the Nigger Hole was another big pool we all liked

to fish when the winter run was in. That was the last place I looked. I had figured if Donkey had a problem, he would end up downstream, and then when I looked up there, there was no need to look anymore. Donkey was tied up in the handline, all wrapped up, around and around and around, like if the line had been straight and he held on and rolled down the bank on top of it. I mean that's what it seemed like. Now how he would have got wrapped up like that and then gotten up into the next pool is beyond me. It would mean he had been dragged or pulled or towed up there. A fish like that would have to be awfully big and strong. And Donkey wasn't the sort to give in easy to anything.

"I got Donkey out of the water and up onto the rocks. He had his arms wrapped around the big cork bobber. He looked like some kind of green otter hugging an abalone. He looked like a wrapped-up package. He looked like an enormous hunk of bait.

"After seeing Donkey was dead like that, I decided to carry him down to the Nigger Hole. I figured that way I could tell everyone I found him there and we could all agree that Donkey must have hooked his big fish and gone into the river fighting it. That would all make sense. That would make us all feel like Donkey had died like any of us would have wanted to. I mean I'm sure he did. How else would he have ended up in the other pool? But then we'd still be arguing how it happened and why. And like Wally said, we've all got better things to think about than that."

Good as Gold
From Sepic's Journals

*I*got ahold of Peter, and he started right in about a hole that had formed where the tidal slough near the Del Mar racetrack empties into the surf. Just off the plane, I burned up most of the day seeing family and negotiating traffic in search of a license. Peter called back from his wife's condo, figured we were still an hour away from the tongue of the flood. In the meantime, he'd tie a sand crab or two. *Yeah, right, Peter.* But by God, we march in through the front door and he's hard at it, looking like a cobbler hunched over his bench.

We got beat up by the surf collapsing at the edge of the trough in front of the riprap hauled in to protect somebody's beachfront dream. Later, a kid on the 101 bridge spotted mullet, and we cast to them, trying to make believe they were something else. But then, Peter spotted a real fish hovering in the clear water of a hole from the remnants of an old piling, its broad pectorals flaring as if the wings of a mallard set to land. Big corbina? Little white sea bass? Peter threw a backcast that nearly snagged an archetypal blonde indigene steering a red import convertible. Distracted, he fumbled a backhand roll cast, lining the fish into oblivion.

Back at the condo, we steered clear of beer. Peter was heading back to Estero Beach, below Ensenada, where he was working on a new trailer between tides. I was pointed beyond the northern reaches of L.A. on this, my first-ever fishing trip to the Southland. Nearly four decades a resident, and now I was a tourist. It was the last place on earth I'd ever imagined I'd visit to go fishing.

My host lives in a cozy inland hamlet that you recognize if you watch movies. Last year, they hung Christmas decorations all along Main Street in July. I had a hamburger for lunch in a diner that hasn't changed since the introduction of saddle shoes, bobby socks, pleated skirts, and tight mohair sweaters. The brick-red wooden train station looks as if it should be doused in billowing steam.

Trout were rising below the house. The stream moved silently through the deep shade of sycamores, and the dry air sharpened the nutty smell of oak trees, chaparral, and memories of canyon fires. Above the ridge to the west hung smudges of maritime clouds. A trout rose again, the shock wave of its tiny retreat sending visceral distortions across the surface of the slick, black pool.

In the morning, I put up a 3-weight. I wouldn't have done it unless my host had encouraged me to try. The stream seemed as precious as museum artwork, the trout in it delicate as Chinese verse. *Fragile*, I kept thinking. I know what this land has been through, too.

One fish would be enough. Okay, two. I built a leader half again as long as the rod. Trout scattered like dust beneath my first cast. The effect was like broken glass falling from a window sash. Empty. The water was so clear, I imagined I could see the silhouette of new blood knots as the shadow of my leader crept along the bottom of the narrow pool. Later, when I found fish that I could drift a tiny nymph to without spooking, they appeared instantaneously at the end of the tippet, like the song of a meadowlark heard through an open window as you drive down a sagebrush highway. This wasn't fishing, it was heart surgery. I threw a gentle loop and watched the fly vanish again, as if a pulse of gold blood in my own veins swung it through an arc beyond my doing.

There's a spot along the highway where corbina like to feed. My host drives this route often, and at a certain post along the seawall, about halfway between the famous surf spot and one of

the old oil-drilling piers, he swings free of traffic, finds a parking
spot, and clamors down the granite riprap for a better, closer
look. This is one of the reasons he has begun to catch corbinas
on flies with a frequency unlike any I've heard of before.
Another reason is that he works at it really hard.

Today, the water is empty, the small surf transparent as
schoolboys' lies. In another half-hour the corbinas might show
up, coursing the shore break and shallows like bats working
through treetops at twilight. I know this game. My host says he's
finally reached the point in his surf fishing where he doesn't
always feel as if he's shooting blindly into a forest, hoping he hits
something. If not always, then *sometimes?* We both gaze out at
the water, squinting between sets and deep sighs.

The famous sportsman's surf cottage is not what you
would expect. They no longer build this small in the West. This
is any place but that, a stretch of coast more renowned among
surfers than any one of them could ever be. In the right light,
you can almost see Baja. By that, I mean these are beaches that
belong to another time, the sculptures unblemished, original,
by hands divine.

Wind was honking out of the north, lifting flecks of foam
off rafts of kelp dislodged by winter surf and warm summer
waters. Surf puddled on the outside reef, then wallowed in and
dumped hard on the sand, smearing seaweed through the shallows. The sweet spot was a hole of conflicting currents not
unlike you would find beneath a waterfall, big enough to park a
yacht. Just days before here, the son of the famous sportsman
had speared a large white sea bass. Despite the wind, surf, and
weed, I liked my chances if I could somehow cast my streamer
a full seventy-five yards.

Short of the mark by most of that distance, I still managed a
hookup. I nursed the fish into view, caught sight of the foggy
gray scales of a corbina, and hollered, rod poised, for my host's

admiration. Calling through the wind, I felt the fish slip free.

It was okay. No it wasn't, but what else is there to say? We ventured overland to another break, a replica of the first, and my host started nailing surfperch. I watched him strike and land several. *Oh, just another perch*, I thought, each time he released one. Then I trotted down the beach and begged him for a fly.

I need to mention here my escape from a tragic religion that attests no man or woman should succumb to sport as lowly as surfperch. I now believe the purpose of perch in the grand scheme of things is to teach all of us how much fun is available in life if we are willing to carry a fly rod across the beach. My host has gone a long way in facilitating that pleasure by fashioning a fly out of little more than a size-6 hook, a pair of small dumbbell eyes, and swags of red marabou. My host calls his surf fly "the Gremmie." That's short for "gremlin." What makes the name feel authentic are the subcultural associations of gremmies as young, inexperienced surfers. As an actual pattern, the Gremmie may or may not last: the sport with fly rods on the coast remains too young, too fresh, too wide open to tell. The size and mechanical properties of the fly—that is, its balance in meeting the needs of casting, sinking, and appearing to swim as if viable foodstuff of the surf—these properties work together in a marriage of functions second to none. Swarms of perch feeding in the shore break help this fly work really well, too.

Perch will never supplant your greatest dreams or deepest desires. Meanwhile, their thumping strike and throbbing runs through waves raked by howling twilight winds may reacquaint you with the kind of giddy sport that full-service accommodations simply do not allow. These are wild animals migrating in the margins of the sea, and nobody is there waiting should the next wave lift you off your feet.

We decided to forgo protocol and kill our dinner. Granted, perch are perch. But out of respect for the famous sportsman, we had spiced his larder with salads and fierce peppers from my host's canyon garden. The tortillas were fresh and flour, the oil virgin, cold-pressed, and sizzling. From the cooler we drew dark, cold drinks and outside watched the wind move through the stars.

The Informer drew my host aside. The details were explicit: high tide, a hole, a shallow channel, two jetties. He was casting to corbinas he could see, said the Informer, and he had had some success.

"What kind of success?"

I lowered the carousels onto the slide projector inside the plastic milk crate along with fly boxes, framed blowups, books. Members of the Sespe Fly Fishers straggled out of the room. I patted the front of my shirt pocket to make sure I hadn't misplaced the check.

"Four-fish-this-week success," said my host. We exchanged looks that said, emphatically, *you could do a lot worse in a season*. I had to drop my eyes when I began to contemplate the number of corbinas I had caught on flies my whole life. "He started fishing corbs nearly two years ago," added my host. "I think these are his first ones."

When we found him the next morning, the Informer looked clearly like a man on a tear. He held a wad of dip inside his lower lip, not to one side, but right in the middle, as if to do him the most good. He had on a T-shirt, board shorts, and a fanny pack, no shoes or wading gear, just the 8-weight he used to point out the setup, where the channel would fill and the direction the corbina would follow, where he'd been standing on casts when he hooked his fish. You could tell he was all over them, like maybe he hadn't been into the office before noon all week, dining on Franco-American and donuts, and his marriage was just going to have to handle this kind of thing or else. When he mentioned needing to quit as soon as the tide peaked to go pick up his son, I thought the or-else stage might have already arrived. We were two hours early, and he had been casting before we arrived. Compared with him, I felt along for the ride.

My host departed for work. I waded the shallows below the mouth of the slot, one eye on the Informer. Now and then he flexed at the knees, going still as a heron, until his face swung with the current as if the bow of a boat affixed to an anchor rope. I imagined bull's-eyes the size of jellyfish awash in the channel, the Informer's fly piercing the surface like song in a breeze. It was his dance. The strike was as inevitable as breath.

They get bigger, but not by a lot. You might like to think size doesn't matter in corbinas, the rarity of the feat of taking them on a fly being what it is. But of course, you know you would be wrong.

The Informer steered the fish through the channel and slid it up onto the sand. He said something inarticulate about sight casting, the edge in his voice rising. He handed me a disposable Instamatic.

When the fish, released, disappeared in the wash, the Informer straightened up and motioned toward the channel. "Right there," he said, pointing with his eyes.

They don't come much better than the Blaster. His casting, he'll tell you, is tops, champion caliber. He's reached the point, in fact, where he would rather cast than fish, he explained. Well, maybe for bonefish. And on the Dean. Behind the reception counter at my host's cabinet shop, the Blaster began to describe the mechanics of competition, guys lined up along an artificial pool, shooting the fly through hoops of various sizes, at various distances, one called "Trout," the other "Bass," and on and on, depending on sizes and distances and enough other variables to challenge a physicist. Perfect scores, said the Blaster, are not only possible, but for victory, required . . . at which point I interrupted and solicited agreement that this sort of thing was absolutely, insanely absurd.

My host shifted his gaze uncomfortably. The Blaster, off balance, backpedaled a thought or two.

"So what kind of rod do *you* like?" he countered.

"What do you mean, 'what *kind* of rod'?" Baffled, I watched my host disappear into his office.

"You know, *what kind?*" repeated the Blaster.

"Well, if I need a five-weight, I build a five-weight. If I need an eight, I build an eight."

The Blaster stared back at me.

"Oh, you mean what *brand?*" I asked.

The bass pond lay precisely where you would put it if you had three hundred acres tucked into the chaparral and scrub-oak foothills beneath the Topatopa mountains. Not more than seventy-five yards across in any direction, the spot felt as private as a bedroom. You try not to ask yourself, *How do I act like I deserve this?* You'd be stoked if you were hunting quail here, too.

The punt, unfortunately, was in use. Two guys explained through a break in the cattails that they knew the property manager. My host got them to agree to give up the boat for the last hour before sunset. I'm not sure how I would have felt about the same request. Later, one of the guys described himself as "white oil-field trash." You can make a lot more out of this scene than I'm going to here.

My host cast a little fly on a five-weight backup rod and hooked a bluegill. That seemed good enough. Then he said, "Look at this." By the time I did, a bass had come halfway out of the pond to swallow the bluegill, and it disappeared like a rock into the weeds below. Overmatched, my host leaned on the bass until breaking it off. I'm pretty sure he pulls this one on all of his guests.

Prime time arrived right on schedule. That afternoon, I'd tied pairs of grizzly hackle dyed green to an old saltwater popper body tinted by felt-tip marker, a spooky concoction that didn't work nearly as well as my host's deer-hair divers launched from his surf-weight rod. Or maybe his casts fell tighter to the reeds. The bass, when moved, exploded like tantrums. We missed most of the strikes, lost to weeds most of the fish we did hook. This time, I'm going to contend that it really didn't matter: a strike like this is as memorable as seaside hail. Of course, I say that because my host landed fish and I didn't. Nobody was counting, but there are facts you can't ignore.

On the morning of my departure, we found the Informer hard at it again. He and my host let me take the slot. It didn't matter. My host and his Gremmie plucked another big corbina out of the inshore wash. That fish alone, I believe, would change the lives of the vast majority of fly fishers in the state. Two weeks later, my host nailed a twelve-pound striper out of a river mouth where a history of such sport on flies simply does not exist. The discoveries feel endless.

In the end, it's all memories, metaphors, moments. I would like to profess a strong moral point of view, but if it hasn't shown yet, I'm lost. A fly-fishing career is a lot of things. A sense of place may be the one that matters. More than the West, this is the coast. I've been warned against value judgments, but here goes. The biggest adventure out there is always close to home.

Sepic's Dream Journal
Final Entry

You would know he's a father. A clearing in the woods reveals a camp on a river, a clear, tumbling stream that is nowhere if not the West, the shadows of heavy fir and cedar spilling through the morning sun. The man steps from a tent, blinking against the light. He goes to a van and taps on a dirtied window, the face of a young retriever rising. She comes out full of herself, her tail a blur, a tall, lean Chesapeake, pressing her big head into his thighs. They move to the edge of the trees and pee, one looking at the other, their expressions remote and alike.

You would know he's a father as he kneels to build a fire, one knee in the dirt, poking through ashes for an ember from the night before. The dog scales him from behind, and he wheels and scolds her, commands her to sit and then lie. He reaches out and scratches her fondly around the ears. He has broad, veiny hands, the strong, knowing fingers of a trades-man or a sportsman or his own father, though this is perhaps only chance. He stacks the kindling in a neat, deliberate pile, attending to each stick like a child building with blocks, with the abrupt, perfunctory glance of a nanny doing laundry. He lowers his face and blows on the smoke. When the flames appear, he turns to the dog and smiles, raising his eyebrows in fun.

The man gazes briefly at the fire, adjusting it here and there, his face returning to a studious look, lost in the moment. It is easy to imagine him the victim of random crime. He has gray eyes that probably were once blue, and the skin around them and up his forehead is blotchy with damage from sun. His hair is cut short and is also gray, an absence of color more than an actual shade. But he is not old, falling instead into that broad span of fatherly life prone to hopeless, benign smiles and to lies, buffoonery, and terror.

The man builds up the fire from a pile of gathered limbs. Those that are too long he sets on a rock of the fire ring and stomps in two. The dog bounds about him, and he looks uncertainly toward the tent. He breaks another branch and hurls it into the river. The dog disappears over the bank, and he listens to her frantic, high-pitched barking. He is still uncertain whether she will bring anything back. He glances again at the tent and believes for a moment he sees an outline stirring. He hurriedly unlatches the lid of a stove, disdaining the noisy pump. He opens the valve and simultaneously strikes a match on the back of a raised thigh of his Levi's, pausing to be pleased with himself as he aims the flame at the wheezing burner.

The dog returns with the stick, and the man praises her, though she comes only as far as the fire before lying down. When she rushes past him, he knows before he sees her that the girl is already there. The dog is instantly upon her, and she grimaces and thrusts out her hands, trying to pet her. She barely keeps her feet. The man approaches, saying nothing, afraid his voice will excite the dog even more. He takes hold of the dog's collar and jerks her forcefully down. He gathers the girl in his arms and lowers himself slowly, coming to rest on one knee, evidence of pain in his eyes. Something is wrong with his back. He calms the dog, running fingers over her brow, speaking softly as she quivers, staring at the child.

You would know he's a father as he holds the girl on his knee, his strong hands gripping her gently. She looks back and forth between the man and the dog, her eyes dark and filled with wonder. She has long, black hair and a rich Latin skin, and the wonder in her eyes speaks of the same pale, hopeless joy as the eyes before her, the man and the dog, the father and his friend. The child reaches out a small, dark hand and touches the dog's face, the tears on the man's cheeks. You would know he's a father as he draws the girl to him, holding the dog at bay.